First World War Trials and Executions

First World War Trials and Executions

Britain's Traitors, Spies and Killers 1914–1918

Simon Webb

PEN & SWORD
HISTORY

First published in Great Britain in 2015 by
Pen & Sword History
an imprint of
Pen & Sword Books Ltd
47 Church Street
Barnsley
South Yorkshire
S70 2AS

ISBN 978 1 47383 397 5

A CIP catalogue record for this book is available from the British
Library

Typeset in Ehrhardt by
Mac Style Ltd, Bridlington, East Yorkshire
Printed and bound in the UK by CPI Group (UK) Ltd,
Croydon, CRO 4YY

Pen & Sword Books Ltd incorporates the imprints of Pen & Sword
Archaeology, Atlas, Aviation, Battleground, Discovery, Family
History, History, Maritime, Military, Naval, Politics, Railways, Select,
Transport, True Crime, and Fiction, Frontline Books, Leo Cooper,
Praetorian Press, Seaforth Publishing and Wharncliffe.

For a complete list of Pen & Sword titles please contact
PEN & SWORD BOOKS LIMITED
47 Church Street, Barnsley, South Yorkshire, S70 2AS, England
E-mail: enquiries@pen-and-sword.co.uk
Website: www.pen-and-sword.co.uk

Contents

Introduction

T his book tells the story of thirty-one trials which took place in this
country during the First World War. In every case, the accused men
were subsequently executed. No woman was executed in Britain
during this period, although in Chapter 4 we shall look at one woman
who was sentenced to death for espionage, but subsequently reprieved. It
is over half a century since anybody was executed in the United Kingdom
and it is easy to forget just how routine and commonplace such events were
throughout much of the twentieth century. Taking a few years at random,
in 1920, twenty-four men and one woman were hanged; in 1928 there were
twenty-six executions, and even as late as 1950, twenty men were hanged.
On average, there was an execution in this country every two or three weeks
between 1900 and 1964.

The number of executions fell slightly during the First World War. In the
period covered by this book, that is to say from the summer of 1914 until he
autumn of 1918, fifty-one men were executed in England. This works out at
about one each month. Most, about 80 per cent, were of course hanged for
murder, but just over a fifth were shot for espionage. In addition to this, one
spy and one traitor were hanged.

There was a unique and grisly fascination about capital trials, which were
quite literally a matter of life and death for the defendant. The frisson of
horror felt when reading about a person being sentenced to death was quite
different from the sensation experienced upon learning that this or that
individual will be spending a certain number of years in prison.

Most non-fiction books about murder focus almost exclusively on the
crimes themselves and sometimes upon the trials which followed. There is
typically only a sentence or two about the ultimate fate of the criminals;
usually, no more than the blunt statement that the person was sent to
prison for so many years or executed on such and such a date. The present

book is different in this respect, in that it details wherever possible the condemned man's experiences after being sentenced to death and recounts what happened in the condemned cell and during the execution itself. This makes, on occasion, for gruesome and harrowing reading.

There were one or two differences between the executions which took place during the First World War and those being carried out before and after the conflict. In the first place, as mentioned above, there were fewer hangings than in peacetime. There was also the fact that the hanging of condemned criminals was supplemented in a dozen or so capital cases by the use of firing squads. This was an unexpected development, it being the custom up until 1914 that the use of military firing squads was undertaken only when the British army was serving overseas and that such executions did not take place in the British Isles. The experimental use of death by shooting did not really catch on and by the time of the next world war had been more or less abandoned. During the Second World War only one German spy was executed by firing squad; the rest being hanged like common murderers.

It might be interesting for readers to know how the use of the death penalty came to be abandoned in the United Kingdom. In addition, it may come as a surprise to learn that it was technically possible to be hanged or shot until eighteen months before the beginning of the twenty-first century.

By the mid 1960s, executing criminals was fast becoming a thing of the past. The use of capital punishment had fallen into abeyance some time before its official abolition. Only three men were hanged in 1962 and 1963, all others who had been sentenced to death being reprieved. The last hangings in the United Kingdom took place in August 1964, when two men were hanged simultaneously in Manchester and Liverpool. Theirs were the only executions that year and the last ever to be carried out in the United Kingdom. Sentences of death have been passed since those final executions in 1964, but there was no chance of their being carried out. As recently as 1992, for instance, Tony Teare was condemned to death after being found guilty of murder on the Isle of Man. There was not the remotest possibility, though, of his being executed and the sentence was almost immediately commuted to imprisonment for life. Theoretically at least, hanging remained the punishment in this country for treason and piracy; a state of affairs which lingered on until very nearly the end of the twentieth century. Three events in 1998 combined finally to put an end to any possible future use of the death penalty.

The first development in 1998 to signal the final end of even the very remote possibility of any future executions taking place was when an amendment was added to the Crime and Disorder Bill making its way through Parliament. This abolished the death penalty for treason and piracy, replacing hanging with life imprisonment. In May that year, Parliament also voted to ratify the sixth amendment of the European Convention on Human Rights, which prohibits the death penalty other than during a war. Even so, there was still a slim chance that at some future date, there could be executions in this country for spying or treachery. This was removed in November 1998, when the Human Rights Act came into force. From that time on, Britain was legally bound not to use the death penalty for any purpose, either now or in the future.

Judicial hanging and shooting have thus been consigned to the status of historical curiosities in this country. Nobody under the age of 60 is even likely to remember hearing or reading about an execution actually taking place in Britain. This will perhaps serve to make the various anecdotes about the condemned cell and scaffold which are contained in this book all the more disturbing.

Chapter One

An Old-Fashioned Way to Die:
The Cut-throat Razor as Murder Weapon

There are fads and fashions in murder, just as there are in other fields of human endeavour, such as architecture and music. Today, the commonest means used in this country to cut short the life of another person is stabbing with a sharp implement. Around 40 per cent of British homicides are carried out in this way. A century ago, rather than jabbing with something pointed, tastes ran more to slashing and hacking; invariably at the throat or neck of the prospective victim. A third of the murderers hanged between the outbreak of war in the summer of 1914 and the signing of the armistice in 1918, committed their crimes by using this method. The weapon wielded was, in almost every such case, an open razor. Not for nothing was the open or 'straight' razor known colloquially as the 'cut-throat' razor!

Murder is usually a spur of the moment act, being committed with whatever weapon lays closest at hand. In America, where privately owned firearms are alarmingly common, two thirds of homicides involve the use of guns. In Britain, a hundred years ago, the most deadly instrument readily available in the average home was the razor.

For centuries, men in this country shaved using single-edged blades which, when not in use, folded neatly into a handle. These razors looked a little like blunt-ended knives. Such open blades can be hazardous, but it wasn't until American inventor King Camp Gillette patented his 'safety razor' in December 1901, that men wishing to be clean shaven had any choice in the matter. The first safety razors appeared in Britain in 1905, but they were slow to catch on and when the First World War started in 1914 most men in this country still relied upon the straight razor.

If there are fashions in murder, then different methods of suicide too fall in and out of favour. Fifty years ago, the most popular way of ending one's life was to pop a shilling in the gas meter, turn on the oven without lighting it and just lay with one's head inside. The replacement of coal gas with natural gas from the North Sea in the early 1970s put an end to this particular method of self-destruction. Another old standby of the hopeful suicide was the same implement which featured in so many murders: the cut-throat razor. Sometimes, the same razor would be used in quick succession, firstly for murder and then for attempted suicide. This was what almost happened with one of the first murders of the 1914–1918 war. This case has several interesting features, not the least of which is that that the hangman who executed the murderer for cutting his wife's throat with a razor, went on to kill himself by cutting his own throat; also using a razor for this purpose.

Charles Frembd: The Oldest Man to be Executed

Hanged at Chelmsford, 4 November 1914

Once upon a time, Leytonstone was a pretty little village in Essex. It was, in the course of time though, overwhelmed by the inexorable growth of the capital and is now an unremarkable and singularly unattractive district in East London. The suburb's only claim to fame is that one or two famous people were born or grew up here; film director Alfred Hitchcock and, more recently, footballer David Beckham being the most well known of these. Just over a century ago, Leytonstone enjoyed brief notoriety as the scene of a brutal murder. This killing was essentially a commonplace, domestic crime. There were however several points of the case which caused it to stand out; not least of which was that the murderer became the oldest person to be hanged in twentieth-century Britain.

In August 1914, Charles Frembd and his wife Louisa were living together at 44 Harrow Road in Leytonstone. The unusual surname is accounted for by the fact that Frembd was of German origin, not a particularly good thing to be in England at that time; the very month that England had declared war on Germany. Although he had been born in Germany, Charles Frembd had not lived there since he was a teenager. At various times he had lived in the United States and different parts of England, before settling down to run a grocer's shop on the ground floor of his home in Harrow Road. Until the previous year, Frembd had been a widower, but while staying at the seaside resort of Yarmouth he met a widow who took his fancy. Despite being in his late sixties, there was a whirlwind courtship and marriage followed in the spring of 1913.

From the beginning, it is possible that Charles Frembd realised that he had made a terrible mistake in remarrying. There were constant arguments and it seems that his wife was often nagging him in front of witnesses. None of which can of course excuse, although it may go some way towards explaining, his actions on the night of Thursday, 27 August 1914. Charles and Louisa Frembd shared their home with a domestic servant by the name of Dorothy Woolmore, who had lived with them since October, 1913. On the night of 27 August, she went to bed at 11:00 pm, leaving the Frembds sitting downstairs. Twenty minutes after retiring, she heard Mrs Frembd going to bed and then, at about 11:50 pm, her husband. According to the evidence which she subsequently gave at Charles Frembd's trial for murder, Dorothy Woolmore heard no sounds at all during the night.

It was Louisa Frembd's habit to wake her servant at 7:30 am each day. On the morning of 28 August, Dorothy Woolmore woke up at 8:20 am and realised that she had overslept. Worried that she would get into trouble, she dressed hurriedly and went downstairs to start cleaning. Finding that her mistress was not up either, the girl, thinking that Mrs Frembd might be ill, went back upstairs and knocked on the bedroom door. There was no answer. Dorothy carried on with her work, but when there was still no sign of either of the Frembds after another half hour, she went upstairs and knocked again on the bedroom door. This time when there was no reply, she pushed open the door. A scene of utter horror greeted her.

Both Charles and Louisa Frembd were in bed; laying side by side. The two of them though were drenched in blood. Charles Frembd had cut his wife's throat, before making an ineffectual attempt to end his own life in the same way. The shocked servant ran to the local police station.

The police found that although Louisa Frembd was dead, her husband had suffered only superficial cuts from his suicide bid. He was removed to hospital for treatment. By the side of the bed, they found a note written by the man whom they strongly suspected of murdering his wife. It said, 'Her first husband made off with himself and I cannot stand it any longer.' They also recovered the open razor which had been used to kill Louisa Frembd.

As soon as Charles Frembd was well enough to be discharged from hospital, he was arrested and charged with both the murder of his wife and also with attempting to commit suicide. This was done as a precaution. In the event that Frembd was acquitted of the murder charge, the police wished to ensure that they had something that they could get him on. It is sometimes forgotten that attempting suicide was a criminal offence in this country until 1961.

Charles Frembd's defence was neither original nor convincing. He claimed to have no memory at all of the events leading up to his wife's death and was unable therefore to offer any explanation of what might have occurred. He did go so far as to say that his wife's nagging had driven him to distraction.

Counsel for Frembd found that the task of defending his client was sabotaged by Charles Frembd himself. The defence was originally to be one of insanity. Sidney Dyer, the Medical Officer at Brixton Prison agreed that Frembd, who was 71, had signs of senile decay; what we would today call dementia or Alzheimer's disease. Frembd though, refused point blank to accept this and insisted on asserting that he was fit to plead and stand trial. It proved impossible to talk the old man out of this disastrous course of action.

The trial was held on 15 October 1914, before Mr Justice Rowlett at London's Central Criminal Court, better known as the Old Bailey. It was little more than a formality, there being no real doubt that it had been Charles Frembd who cut his wife's throat. The jury did however add a rider to their verdict of guilty, recommending mercy for Frembd on account of his age and apparent infirmity. Nobody really expected a man of that age to be hanged.

Unfortunately, two factors militated against Charles Frembd having his sentence commuted to imprisonment. The first of these was the utterly ruthless nature of his crime. This had not been a death resulting from a violent struggle, but the killing of a defenceless woman as she lay in her bed. The second point working against Frembd was of course the fact that he was German. Anti-German sentiments were beginning to catch hold in Britain and having of an obviously foreign name, combined with the misfortune to have been born in Germany probably didn't help his chances of evading the gallows. That some anti-German prejudice was at work may be seen from the newspaper coverage of the case. *The Times*, for instance, reported that the Home Secretary was not going to grant a reprieve for Frembd under the headline, 'NO REPRIEVE FOR THE GERMAN MURDERER'.

The execution of Charles Frembd was notable for another reason, apart from his being the oldest person to be hanged in twentieth-century Britain. Because Leytonstone was at that time in Essex, Frembd was held under sentence of death in Springfield Prison in Chelmsford; it being the invariable practice at that time to execute murderers in the county in which they had committed their murder. His was to be the last execution ever carried out in Essex, because the gaol was a few weeks later handed over to the military for the duration of the war. The gallows were dismantled and never again erected.

Charles Frembd was hanged on 4 November, the executioner being John Ellis, who carried out all but eight of the forty executions by hanging which took place in this country during the First World War. Ironically, in view of the number of men he hanged who had wielded open razors as their weapon of choice with which to commit murder, Ellis later died after cutting his own throat with a razor, following his retirement as chief hangman. Details of his life and death are to be found in Appendix 1.

John Ellis decided to give the condemned man a drop of six feet and six inches. There were frequent disagreements between the executioner and the prison authorities over the length of the drop which should be given during an execution. The background to these disputes is outlined in Appendix 3. Briefly stated, hanging a person involved a very fine calculation which would ideally snap the neck cleanly. Too little and the victim might choke to death; too long a drop and the head might be entirely detached from the body.

Charles Frembd's execution was marred by an unfortunate incident. When Ellis had seen him on the day before the execution, he had noticed that Frembd looked unwell. His throat was still surgically plastered from his suicide attempt and this worried the executioner. Hanging men with injuries to their throat was apt to be a messy business and more than one condemned man had been reprieved on those grounds alone; hanging him might reopen the wound with all the gory consequences. As it happened, the mishap which occurred during the execution had nothing to do with Frembd's injuries.

The grim procession of prison governor, chaplain, warders, executioner and condemned man moved to the gallows on the morning of 4 November without incident; the old man appearing to be dazed and scarcely aware of what was going on. Once on the trapdoor, Ellis swiftly pulled the white cotton hood over the doomed man's head and secured the noose around his neck. The executioner then moved to the lever which operated the trapdoors. As he turned, Frembd fainted and began falling to one side. This meant that as the trap opened, he did not drop vertically down, but fell to one side. At the inquest, it was noticed that the dead man's face had a number of injuries, including a black eye. These had been caused by his hitting the trapdoors as he plummeted through them.

There are a number of similarities between the case of Charles Frembd and that of John Eayres, whom we shall next be looking. The wives of both men had previously been married, the precipitating factor in both murders being the nagging of their wives and both men used open razors to kill their victims. Both murderers also tried to cut their own throats soon after killing their wives. The two murders and executions were separated in time by less than a week.

John Eayres: A Row about a Halfpenny

Hanged at Northampton, 10 November, 1914
We shall in this book be looking at a number of murders which were committed for astonishingly trivial reasons, but the death of Sarah Ann Eayres on 22 August 1914, must surely be in a class of its own. This was a murder committed as a result of a row about ownership of a halfpenny!

Sarah Ann Weldon was a widow who, in 1911, married 56-year-old John Eayres; a tinsmith from Peterborough. They settled down in a house at 4 School Place in Peterborough and from the beginning their life together was marked by quarrelling and strife. Part of the problem was that both husband and wife were heavy and immoderate drinkers and prone to drunken squabbles.

William Rodgers, who lived next door to the Eayres in School Place, heard the couple arguing at about 5:30 pm on 22 August. A little later, their quarrel became a physical fight and another witness saw them rolling around on the pavement outside their house, punching and scratching each other. Later that evening, Mr and Mrs Eayres were seen in the centre of Peterborough, where a third witness, Thomas Hawksworth, spoke to John Eayres. It appeared that earlier that day, a halfpenny had been found in the house and both John Eayres and his wife claimed ownership of it. It was this which had sparked the row. The old halfpenny was the second smallest denomination of British coins at that time and was worth, in modern currency, about a fifth of 1p!

Later that day, groaning was heard from the yard at the back of the Eayres' house. William Rodgers was urged by his wife to investigate and when he did so, he found John Eayres laying on his back, covered in blood. In the outside toilet was his wife. She was dead, having had her throat cut with such ferocity that her head was nearly severed from her body. Closer examination revealed that John Eayres had made a half-hearted attempt to cut his own throat. Significantly, although he had used an open razor to cut his wife's throat, when it came to his own; he was more cautious. Instead of a razor, he had used a blunt penknife to inflict a number of superficial scratches on the side of his neck. The blood in which his clothes were soaked was nearly all Sarah Ann's.

The similarities between the murders committed by John Eayres and Charles Frembd are quite uncanny. They extend to the defence offered by both men: that they could not remember the murder itself. When questioned by the police, Eayres told them that he certainly recalled arguing with his wife, but the last thing he could remember clearly was that she had hurled the sugar basin at him, which had struck him on the nose. After that, everything was a complete blank. It was with this unpromising material that his defence counsel tried to save John Eayre's neck from the gallows.

At his trial for murder before Mr Justice Avory, John Eayres' defence team put forward the theory that the charge should really be one of manslaughter, on the grounds that the crime had been committed in the heat of the moment and with no malice beforehand. It was an ingenious idea, but unfortunately for Eayres, the judge was not impressed. He pointed out that if a person lashed out on the spur of the moment in response to some provocation and death resulted; that could indeed be a case of manslaughter. This was quite different to what had befallen Sarah Ann Eayres. Her husband must have gone off in search of a weapon which he intended to use upon her. This indicated a degree of premeditation which could not possibly be consistent with a verdict of manslaughter. It surprised nobody when the jury brought in a verdict of murder and Eayres was duly sentenced to death.

When John Ellis went to Northampton to hang Eayres, it was to be the hundredth execution which he had carried out. He observed that Eayres looked very depressed; as well he might under the circumstances. On the morning of the execution, Ellis entered the condemned man's cell and saw that he had been crying. As he was led out of the cell towards the coach house where the gallows had been erected, Eayres began sobbing again. He had a slight limp, which made the progress of the procession slow and halting. When they reached the gallows, John Eayres stopped dead. Then he said in a low voice, 'I'm going to die for a bad woman'. In another few seconds, he was dead.

Frank Steele: 'I cut her throat with that razor on Sunday afternoon'

Hanged at Durham, 11 August 1915

One of the most shocking aspects of the murders carried out with cut-throat razors during the First World War is that nearly all were committed by men, against women. Even worse is the number of such killings which were carried out while the victim was laying in bed, obviously not anticipating a deadly assault. In other words, these were not spur-of-the-moment crimes, where a fight escalated into ever greater violence, until murder was done. These were women laying peacefully in their beds, whose husbands or lovers approached them unawares and slashed open their throats. We have already looked at one such murder, that committed by Charles Frembd. Another feature of this kind of murder is that after cutting a woman's throat with great ferocity, these murderers often made feeble and ineffective attempts to end their own lives in the same way; by cutting their own throats. The year following Frembd's and Eayre's executions saw a murder case with many similarities to those committed by these two killers; that of Frank Steele.

Sexual licence and one-parent families are not a product of the swinging sixties; both have been with us throughout recorded history. Despite the impression we sometimes have of Edwardian Britain as being a starchy and repressed society, there was no shortage of unmarried mothers in those days.

One of these was Nana Barrett; a 20-year-old woman who, on the outbreak of war in August 1914, was living in the northern town of Gateshead.

Nana Barrett was pregnant by a man called Joseph Bell and in the autumn of 1914 gave birth to a fine baby boy. Bell was not inclined to support the mother of his child and there was a distinct coolness between them when she went to live with her friend, Elizabeth Gray, at 33 Nelson Street, Gateshead. According to a statement which Elizabeth Gray later made to the police, she strongly suspected that at the time when Nana Barrett and her newborn baby moved in with her, the single mother was earning her living by prostitution.

Nana Barrett went to live at 33 Nelson Street in December, 1914. Within a matter of weeks, two significant events had occurred in her life. The first was that she had struck up an intimate relationship with 28-year-old Frank Steele, who lived next door, at No 31. Then, soon after the two young people became lovers, Barrett's baby died. It was at about this time that she actually moved in with her new boyfriend.

For the first three months, everything went well enough between Frank Steele and Nana Barrett, whom he knew, incidentally, as Nana Spoors. The couple lived together as husband and wife, with no evidence of arguments or friction. In early May, a neighbour of Nana Barrett's who lived at 29 Nelson Street, had seen Nana in the street. She had been weeping and the neighbour, Mary Murphy, had asked what was wrong. Although everybody in the street had seen Nana Barrett with her baby, and most knew that she was unmarried, this was the first time that she revealed who the father was. It was, she told Mary Murphy, a man called Joseph Bell who worked at the Union Hospital in Gateshead. The reason for her distress was that she had recently written to Bell, only for the letter to be returned to her, marked 'Unknown at this address'. It was this action on Nana's part which was to precipitate the train of events which would culminate two weeks later in her death.

Unfortunately for the young woman living at 31 Nelson Street, her partner Frank thought nothing of searching through her belongings and even reading her private correspondence. So it was that some time in May, he came across the letter which had been returned by the Post Office and read it with astonishment which turned to anger. In the letter, written by the woman he loved, she told Joseph Bell that she missed him and urged him to visit her. She explained that the man with whom she lived worked night shifts and that it would therefore be better if Bell came to see her after dark, when Frank Steele was out of the house.

Frank Steele was both a very jealous man and also an exceedingly heavy drinker. These two traits of his character combined fatally on the afternoon of Sunday 16 May 1915. At about noon that day, Elizabeth Gray saw Nana Barrett standing at the door of her house. At 3:00 pm, she heard Frank Steele and Nana Barrett talking. Their voices were not raised and everything seemed quite normal. An hour and three quarters later, an acquaintance of Steele's called William Johnson happened to bump into him in town. Frank Steele was clearly the worse for wear through drink and told Johnson that he had, 'Done Nana in.' William Johnson did not take this statement seriously, although he noticed that there was some kind of wound on Steele's neck.

The following morning, Monday 17 May, Elizabeth Gray saw Frank Steele standing at the door of his house. She remarked that the landlord was coming down the street and would no doubt be collecting the rent that morning. Steele went back into the house and she later heard the landlord knocking at next door, but receiving no answer. At 11:00 am, Elizabeth Gray saw Steele striding down the street. She noticed that the blinds were still down in his house, which struck her as slightly odd. Several times that day, she knocked on the door, but there was no sign of Nana. She assumed that her friend must have gone away for a while.

Frank Steele had gone to visit his mother, who lived at 4 Rye Hill in Newcastle, on the other side of the River Tyne. He was, as his mother was later to put it, 'Wild with drink' when he arrived at her home. He said something about having committed a murder, but was almost incoherent, so much had he drunk. His mother did not know what to make of this confession, but felt uneasy to be in her son's presence. She went upstairs and stayed out of his way until he left the house.

The next day, Tuesday 18 May, Steele turned up again at his mother's house. He was drunk on this visit too and repeated his confession to having murdered somebody. He asked his mother to fetch a police officer, which she did. Police constable Samuel Weir did not know what to make of the rambling drunk, but took him to Westgate police station. When he was searched, a straight razor was found in a case in his pocket. It was heavily stained with blood. Steele said, 'I cut her throat with that razor on Sunday afternoon. She came in drunk. I done it.' He continued, 'I went to bed in the house and slept all night. I intended to finish myself tonight.'

After locking Frank Steele in a cell, Sergeant James Forsyth went with another officer to investigate the confession which they had heard. There was no reply to their repeated knocking at the door of 31 Nelson Street, so they kicked down the door. Inside, they found a woman laying on a bed, with a pillow covering her face. When they removed this, they discovered that she was dead. Her throat had been cut and blood had soaked the bed and also pooled on the carpet. At the subsequent autopsy, it was found that the wound was clean and straight and that the dead woman had no 'defence' wounds on her hands and arms, such as one might expect to see if the attack on her had been during a struggle or fight. All the indications were that she had been laying peacefully on the bed and somebody had come up and, without warning, slashed open her throat, causing her to bleed to death at once.

When the police returned to Westgate police station and told Steele that he would be charged with the murder of the woman called Barrett, his only response was to remark, 'Spoors, that is what I thought they called her.' He then made a full confession, explaining what had led up to the murder. On 19 May 1915, Frank Steele appeared in the Newcastle police court, charged with murder. There were various other appearances, at the magistrates' court and then the inquest, before he found himself in the dock at the Durham Assizes on 6 July 1915. The trial was presided over by Mr Justice Ridley.

Steele's barrister, S. O. Rowan Hamilton, found himself with a difficult task. He was defending a client who had made no secret of having killed the victim and who had made a long and detailed sworn statement to the police in which he admitted responsibility for the death of Nana Barrett or 'Spoors', as he knew her. Elizabeth Gray and Mary Murphy both gave evidence, which tended to show that the accused man had had a serious grudge against the woman with whom he lived; a grudge connected with the dead woman contacting her previous boyfriend. The police surgeon confirmed that he had examined the scene of the crime and that there was no sign of any struggle. It looked as though the attack on Nana Barrett had been carried out while she was laying, relaxed, on the bed.

The defence advanced by Steele's counsel was that his client had been so hopelessly drunk that he had been unable to form the intention to commit murder. If he hadn't known what he was doing at the time, then it was not possible for him to be a murderer, which by its very nature suggest a deliberate act of killing. According to Rowan Hamilton, the correct verdict for the jury to arrive at, could only be one of manslaughter. This defence is still tried from time to time to this day, but almost invariably without success. Obviously, Frank Steele had chosen to become drunk and could not absolve himself of any of the subsequent events, simply because he had set out to become intoxicated.

After Mr Justice Ridley summed up the case in a notably fair and impartial way, the jury retired to consider their verdict. An hour and a half later, they returned, seeking guidance from the judge. They wished to know the extent to which the consumption of alcohol might be regarded as a mitigating factor. The judge explained to them that while drink alone could not excuse a crime, if they were sure that the man in the dock had been so intoxicated that he had not known what he was doing and could not foresee the results of his actions, then this would make the killing of Nana Barrett manslaughter, rather than murder. Ten minutes after receiving this advice, the jury returned again; this time with their verdict. They found Steele guilty of murder and he was sentenced to death.

The decision which the jury made was probably the correct one; both legally and as a matter of common sense. Can we really imagine a man who was so drunk that he failed to realise that cutting open his girlfriend's neck with a razor would result in serious harm and most likely death?

Frank Steele appealed against the death sentence, but there were no real grounds for doing so. On 11 August 1915, he was hanged in Durham prison. John Ellis, who carried out the execution, might have bungled the task. It was noticed that after the hanging, Steele's face was badly bruised and discoloured, leading to the suspicion that he might have died from asphyxiation and not from the clean fracture of the neck which was aimed at.

The victims of those men hanged for cutting somebody's throat with a razor were almost invariably women, most generally their wives or sweethearts. Once in while though there were occasions when a man would attack another man with a razor. Such a case took place near Liverpool in 1915 and it was notable too for the fact that it ended with a double execution, of two men who had both committed similar crimes but were quite unknown to each other. Sheer coincidence led to their sharing the scaffold in December 1915.

John Thornley and Young Hill: A Double Execution

Hanged together at Liverpool, 1 December 1915
Double executions, with two people hanged simultaneously, side by side, were exceedingly grim affairs. In order to minimise the chance of any mix-ups or errors, the two condemned prisoners were brought to the scaffold one at a time, which meant that one of them would arrive in the execution chamber to be greeted by the sight of a man standing on the trapdoor, hooded and with a rope around his neck. It was absolutely essential that each of the condemned prisoners was placed beneath the specified noose. The necessary drops had previously been calculated to the inch and any confusion might have led to somebody being given too long a drop or not enough to cause instant death.

For the first victim to arrive at the scaffold, there was the awful experience of standing with a rope around his neck for a minute or more, waiting for the second prisoner to be brought from his cell and for the drop then to fall. All of this could be enough to precipitate hysterics or fainting fits; which is precisely what happened at Liverpool's Walton prison on 1 December 1915, when two men were executed together for committing two separate but similar murders. Both had cut their victims' throats.

Some murders are committed for the most trifling of motives. In a case at which we have already looked, a dispute over the ownership of a halfpenny was enough to cause a murder. Incredibly, savage murders have taken place for even feebler excuses than that. There can seldom have been less cause for one man to take the life of another than when a black American sailor called Young Hill killed a crewmate in a dispute over the cleanliness of a bucket.

Young Hill came from Wilson, Louisiana. He was a 28-year-old muleteer on the SS *Antillian*, which left New Orleans for Liverpool on 6 July 1915. Hill's job was to take care of the mules on board, which duty he undertook in a satisfactory way as the ship crossed the Atlantic. On 25 July, the SS Antillian arrived in British waters and unloaded some cargo at Avonmouth, the Bristol port. Twenty-four hours later, the ship was waiting in the Mersey to dock at Liverpool. One circumstance which should be mentioned is that it was the custom on American ships that when there was a crew of mixed races and nationalities, razors would be confiscated for the duration of the voyage and only handed back to their owners when the journey was over. This was to avert precisely the type of crime which was committed on this occasion within a matter of hours of the razors being returned to the men.

While the SS *Antillian* was waiting to dock at Liverpool, a sailor called Crockett was laying ill in his bunk. He asked Young Hill to fetch him some water to drink. Hill went off and returned with a slop bucket, pouring the sick man a drink from that. This was too much for another black sailor called James Crawford. He remarked that he had washed his feet in the bucket earlier that day and that nobody should have to drink such dirty water. He went off to get some clean water for the man who had asked for a drink. This simple act of charity appeared for some reason to enrage Young Hill, because when Crawford returned with fresh water, Hill leaped upon him from behind, pulled back his head and cut the man's throat with a razor.

Crawford broke free and staggered off, blood pouring from a deep wound, which had opened his jugular vein. His assailant ran after him and then slashed again at the wounded man, killing him on the spot. After dealing so savagely with one man, Hill announced that if anybody came near him, he would cut off their head; a threat which, in view of what had so recently happened, nobody on board felt disposed to treat lightly. The ship's captain, Captain Gittins, broke out the revolver which was kept for emergencies and armed with this, he and the Chief Officer tackled the killer and deprived him of the razor with which he had just committed a dreadful murder. A few hours later, the SS *Antillian* docked at Huskisson Dock and Hill was handed over to the police. He told the police who arrested him, 'I have cut a man and they say he is dead.'

When he was brought to trial at the Liverpool Assizes on 29 October that year, Young Hill's defence was that he had been attacked by James Crawford and had only used the razor to defend himself. Three sailors who were present, gave evidence that this was not at all what had happened. Leslie Rucker, Louis Keys and Lorenzo Sullivan all said that the attack on the dead man had been unprovoked. The members of the jury were not impressed with Hill's story and preferred to believe the other witnesses who were present that day. A verdict of guilty was swiftly brought in, although the jury recommended mercy, due to the fact that Hill was not British.

When Mr Justice Ridley asked Hill, in the customary fashion, whether there was any reason why sentence of death should not be passed upon him, the prisoner became agitated and shouted out that nobody should be put to death unless he was sick. He then added, ironically for a man who had been convicted of such a vicious murder, that he didn't believe in putting people to a violent death. After sentence of death had been pronounced and he was being removed from the dock, Hill shouted out that Christ had also been falsely accused and sentenced to death.

An appeal was heard in London, on 15 November 1915, before the Lord Chief Justice, Lord Avory. By sheer coincidence, Hill's appeal was heard on the same day as that of another man who had been condemned to death for murder after cutting someone's throat. John Thornley, the other man appealing against his conviction that day, was a somewhat tragic figure whose crime had been motivated by an obsession which had developed from his love for a young woman.

Thornley was a 26-year-old lamp-man at Macclesfield station, in Cheshire. For something over two years, he went out with Frances Johnson, who was a couple of years younger than him. They eventually became formally engaged, although shortly afterwards there was a quarrel and Frances returned her engagement ring to Thornley. Unable to accept that their relationship was at an end, he took to following her footsteps when she was out and about, together with calling at her house so frequently that in the end her father told him that he must keep away from his daughter.

In September 1915, Frances Johnson's mother and father went on their annual holiday to Cleethorpes, leaving the 24-year-old mill worker alone in the house. For company, she invited the daughter of a neighbour to come and stay in the house with her. Mary Warren worked at the same mill as Frances and the two young women enjoyed having the house to themselves. They went out several times in the evening, including on Friday 17 September, visiting the local theatre. While there, they saw John Thornley, but didn't speak to him.

Mary Warren later explained in detail what had happened after they returned to Frances's house that night. After going to bed – they were sleeping in separate rooms – Mary was awoken in the middle of the night by hearing somebody crashing about in the yard at the back of the house. She then heard the rattle of a downstairs window being raised, followed by footsteps on the stairs. Then there was silence for a short time, followed by a terrible scream. She heard her friend calling for her, but was too terrified to move or go to Frances's aid.

The frightened young woman lay in the darkness for some considerable time, before plucking up courage to get out of bed, throw up the window and call for help in the street. Luckily, three men were passing the house, one of whom happened to be her brother-in-law. Mary rushed downstairs and let them into the house. It did not take them long to discover that Frances Johnson was dead, laying in her bed with her throat cut. By the side of her was a note, which said, 'Dear Ma and Pa. I told you I would kill or cure Frances. I have done it. I hope you will forgive me for breaking God's law.' This note was in John Thornley's handwriting.

The police had no doubt who was responsible for the murder and made it known that they were very anxious to speak to John Thornley. Not only had he left a note by the side of his victim, he had, after killing her, gone downstairs to the kitchen, turned on the light and written other letters in which he admitted his guilt. After leaving the house, Thornley made his way to the beginning of the Pennine Hills, seven or eight miles away, and wandered about there for the whole of Saturday. He slept rough that night and then in the morning, called at a farmhouse, where he begged some food. When the owner of the farm saw Thornley drinking from a cattle trough, he thought that this might be the man for whom the police were searching. He contacted the police, who came and arrested the wanted man.

John Thornley was tried at Chester. He pleaded not guilty by reason of temporary insanity, a defence which the jury rejected. He was convicted and sentenced to death, following which an appeal was made.

Following the failure of the appeals of Young Hill and John Thornley on 15 November 1915, both men were removed to Liverpool's Walton prison to await execution. In the normal way of things, Thornley would have been executed at the Cheshire county prison at Knutsford, but this establishment, like that of Springfield in Chelmsford, had been handed over to the army for the duration of the war.

There was only one condemned cell at Walton prison, which was given to Young Hill. Thornley was lodged in the prison hospital. John Ellis, the executioner, saw an opportunity to make a little extra money from the unusual circumstances of the double execution which he was called upon to conduct at Liverpool. He customarily received £10, plus travelling expenses, for a single execution and £15 for a double one. In this case, he argued, because the two men were from different counties, he should get £20 for the execution, rather than the usual £15. The Sheriff's office in Lancashire did not agree and wrote back to Ellis, saying:

> An execution of two men from different counties in the prison being most uncommon and to us unique, we have, to make sure about the right amount to pay you, been in communication with the Treasury as to what should be paid to you, and, as we anticipated, the reply is that it constitutes an ordinary double execution, and that £15 and expenses is the proper payment.

It had been a valiant attempt, but Ellis was going to get his usual fee and not a penny more.

The actual mechanics of the two executions were complicated by the fact that the condemned men were in different parts of the prison. There was also the question of Hill's mental stability. He had been extremely depressed since the rejection of his appeal and warders feared that he might struggle or otherwise cause trouble when the time came to lead him to the gallows. The prison doctor suggested that it might be necessary, if he collapsed at the last moment, to carry Hill to his execution in a chair, an idea that Ellis thought impractical.

At 7:30 on the morning of the execution, John Thornley was taken from the hospital and placed in a cell nearer to the execution chamber. Half-an-hour later, Ellis entered the cell and strapped the young man's hands behind his back and opened the collar of his shirt, in order that the noose could be fitted easily around his neck. He noticed while doing so that Thornley had a number of tattoos, including one of a heart around the name 'Frances'. After pinioning Thornley, the executioner went to the condemned cell and did the same to Young Hill, who seemed to be in a daze.

When he returned to Thornley to lead him to the gallows, Ellis found that the condemned man had worked his hands loose from the leather strap and expressed a desire to shake hands one last time with the warders who had been guarding him. This was allowed, following which Ellis led Thornley to the scaffold, where an assistant strapped the man's ankles together while Ellis pulled the hood over his head and placed the rope around his neck. It was at this point that Ellis's second assistant brought Hill to the gallows; who was therefore confronted by the sight of a man standing with a noose around his neck, about to die. Such a sight would be likely to disconcert the bravest of men and is not to be wondered at that Young Hill began shaking violently and could hardly be persuaded to walk forward.

Once Hill was standing next to Thornley on the trap doors, Ellis pulled the hood over his head, whereupon Hill cried, 'Thank God!' and promptly began to faint. A warder stepped forward to support the barely conscious man, but when he took Hill's arm to hold him up, Hill let out a piercing shriek, which all of those present found very harrowing. When the rope was placed around his neck, Hill fainted dead away and Ellis quickly pulled the lever and sent both men to their death.

Frederick Holmes: An Unhappy Threesome

Hanged in Manchester, 8 March 1916

There is, it seems, something inherently unstable about sexual relationships involving more than two people. Sooner or later, jealousy rears its head and the arrangement dissolves in acrimony. When one or more of those involved in such setups is addicted to strong drink, the dissolution of the partnership sometimes descends into violence. Such was the case with Frederick Holmes, who shared with several other men the affections of 38-year-old Sarah Woodall.

Sarah Woodall lived what would in those days have been called a 'loose' life. She was married, but had not seen her husband for four years. In the autumn of 1915, she was living in Manchester at 64 Higher Ardwick. Sarah had two particular male friends and, as far as can be made out, divided her attentions pretty equally between the two of them. One was 44-year-old Frederick Holmes and the other a man called George Wake. Sarah Woodall's relationship with Frederick Holmes was that they were lovers. The part that George Wake played is less clear. He maintained to some that his friendship with Sarah was purely platonic, but later events cast doubt upon this claim.

In October, Sarah Woodall's mother, who had been living in the Yorkshire town of Doncaster, died. Her daughter went home for the funeral and discovered that she had inherited about £300 from her mother; a not inconsiderable sum of money in those days. When she returned to Manchester, she invited Frederick Holmes to move in with her and the two of them lived as husband and wife. This arrangement was short lived, because a few days later, George Wake turned up one lunchtime in a pub where she was drinking with an acquaintance called Maude Barker. The three of them drank on and off for the rest of the day and by the time evening came, Sarah decided that she would sooner be with George than Frederick. It is worth mentioning here that there might have been a little more going on here than at first met the eye. Sarah Metcalfe had a conviction for soliciting as a prostitute and her invitation to George Wake might very well have had a financial element. At any rate, at 9:00 that evening, Sarah and George, both a little the worse for wear, arrived back at her home in Higher Ardwick. When Frederick Holmes, with whom she was supposedly now living, answered the door, Sarah shouted at him to get out.

When Frederick Holmes realised what was happening and that he had apparently been supplanted in the affections of Sarah Metcalfe by the man standing next to her, he flew into a rage and attacked George Wake. There was no doubt that Holmes was getting the better of the contest, when Sarah picked up a shovel from the fireplace and whacked him around the head with it. Although momentarily stunned, he continued to assault Wake, knocking him to the floor and even biting him. Seeing that the man she had brought home was getting the worst of the fight, Sarah Metcalfe ran into the street and began shouting, 'Help! Murder! Police!' Not wishing to get into trouble with the police, Frederick Holmes fled at this point and George Wake spent the night at the house.

It might perhaps be thought that a scene such as this would mark the end of most relationships, but Sarah Metcalfe and Frederick Holmes were made of sterner stuff than the average person. Only a few brief weeks later, they agreed to give living together another try and rented a new room at

13 Clifford Street, moving in on Wednesday, 15 November 1915. The house, in Chorton-on-Medlock, Manchester, was owned by a woman called Ellen Weller. A week's rent was paid in advance and it was agreed that in future the sum was to be paid weekly, every Wednesday.

Nobody knows how things were going between the man and woman living together in the front room of 13 Clifford Street. A fortnight after they moved in, Mrs Weller called for the rent on 8 December, but nobody seemed to be at home. The next day, she called again and when there was still no answer to her repeated knocking, she used her duplicate key to enter the room. The blinds were drawn and the room was in darkness. When Mrs Weller raised the blinds, letting daylight flood into the room, she received a tremendous shock. Laying in the bed, with only her head visible, was Sarah Metcalfe. The bedclothes were saturated with blood and there was a large puddle of dried blood beneath the bed as well. It was obvious the woman in the bed was dead. Without wasting any time, Mrs Weller rushed round to the local police station to report what could only be murder or suicide.

At five to one that afternoon, Superintendent Taylor and Sergeant Singleton of the Manchester police arrived at the house in Clifford Street to begin their investigations. They observed that the dead woman had two cuts, one incomparably more serious than the other. There was a cut on her forehead, just above her right eye, but this was relatively trivial. The wound from which she had died was an enormous gash in the right side of her neck. This cut had passed through every part of the throat and neck, penetrating as far as the spinal cord. When Dr Heslop, the police surgeon, arrived, he at once gave it as his opinion that the woman in the bed had died from massive blood loss after having her throat cut so ferociously that her head was almost severed from her body.

It did not take long to rule out suicide as the cause of death, because there was no weapon laying near at hand. Having established that they were dealing with a case of murder, it was not difficult to fix upon a suspect. Both Mrs Weller and the other people living in the house knew that the dead woman had been living with somebody they believed to be her husband. There was no sign of this man and so finding Frederick Holmes became almost at once the main focus of the investigation.

At the same time Dr Heslop arrived on the scene, another police officer turned up. Detective Sergeant George Allen obtained a description of the man who had been living with the murdered woman and then began scouring the nearby streets in search of him. His strategy paid off, because a few hours later, he bumped into the wanted man in nearby Copeland Street. Holmes admitted his identity at once and after being cautioned and arrested, made the following statement on the way to the police station:

It's all right, I could see it coming. I could not have stayed away from her for much longer. I was going to have a drink and then I might have given myself up. It's no use running away.

Once Sergeant Allen and his prisoner reached the police station in Cavendish Street and it was found that Frederick Holmes was openly acknowledging his responsibility for the death of Sarah Woodall he was charged with her murder.

When the charge was being read to him, that he had murdered the woman with 'malice aforethought', in the old form of words used in such cases, he shook his head and protested. 'No malice aforethought,' he said irritably, 'You can cross them two words out!' A mistake was made when drawing up the charge, in that Sarah's name was given as Alice. Holmes pointed this out to the station sergeant who was reading out the charge.

On 13 December the inquest was held into Sarah Woodall's death and the jury brought in a verdict that she had been murdered by Holmes. This proceeding, whereby the jury at an inquest could name the person they believed was responsible for a death, continued until relatively recently; notwithstanding the fact that it was prejudicial to the subsequent trial. The last time that a jury was allowed to name the person whom they supposed to be the murderer was at the inquest in 1974 into the death of Sandra Rivett, the young woman whom many believe to have been killed by Lord Lucan.

On 18 February 1916, Frederick Holmes appeared before Mr Justice Bailhache at the Manchester Assizes, charged with the wilful murder of Sarah Woodall. As the trial progressed, it became apparent that the dead woman had been living what her husband described as an 'immoral life' for some years. It was what had led to their separation. Sarah's friend Maud

Barker gave evidence that the dead woman had been scared of Holmes and that he had threatened to kill her. Detective Constable Frederick George deposed that when he was left alone with the prisoner, Holmes had said, 'After we got in the house, there was the usual haggling. She's a very jealous woman. I think I did it with the razor that I have here in my pocket.' The defence sought to have this statement struck from the record, on the grounds that it was made before any caution had been given to Holmes at the police station.

There was very little for the defence to work on; it not being disputed that Frederick Holmes had cut his girlfriend's throat, so killing her. Nevertheless, some effort was made to portray the crime as either self defence or, failing that, some kind of crime of passion. Holmes made a statement to the court, in which he said that she had been violent and frequently drunk. On the day that she was killed, there had been a furious quarrel and Sarah Woodall had thrown something at him. He had picked up the nearest object and then lashed out at her, only realising too late that it had been a cut-throat razor in his hand as he struck at her. According to Holmes, he had been horrified to find that he had injured the woman he loved so severely. He had tried to offer her religious consolation, by saying, 'You are going to heaven. Pray!'

After she had died, Frederick Holmes claimed that he had laid Sarah carefully in the bed and pulled the sheets over her. He also said that he had spent the night next to her corpse, having placed the dead woman's arm over his chest. None of this impressed the jury, who took only 30 minutes to convict him of murder. He was then sentenced to death.

There was no appeal and Frederick Holmes placed his hopes on the possibility of a reprieve and commutation of the death sentence to one of penal servitude for life. The problem was though that all the forensic evidence suggested that his story about the circumstances of the murder was a pack of lies. Sarah Woodall had in all probability been attacked while she lay in bed and had her throat cut without being given any chance to defend herself.

John Thompson: The Murderous Shepherd

Hanged at Leeds, 27 March 1917

The great majority of murders involving open razors took place in a domestic setting. That, after all, is where one expect to find a razor; in the bathroom or kitchen of somebody's home. Under such circumstances, there is always the possible defence that the implement was snatched up unthinkingly in a blind rage. Courts seldom look favourably upon stories of that sort, but it is at least possible to try. When a straight razor is used in an attack in the open air, the possible explanations for carrying such dangerous article about with one are greatly reduced. When a murder is committed with a cut-throat razor in a farmyard at lunchtime, we can be fairly sure that the person responsible had equipped himself with the murder weapon beforehand and that a degree of premeditation is very likely.

John Henry Tindale was a farm bailiff and he lived at the remote Constitution Hill Farm at Molesworth, not far from Beverley in Yorkshire. Tindale supervised a number of workers, including labourers and shepherds; all of whom ate their mid-day meal in the kitchen of the farmhouse which Tindale and his family occupied.

At about 1:00 pm on 15 February 1917, Tindale observed his 13-year-old daughter Lily entering the stack yard. Half an hour later, the gong was sounded to summon the workers from the fields around the farmhouse and let them know that it was time to eat. It was noticed that one of the men working on the farm, 43-year-old shepherd John Thompson, did not come to the kitchen for his meal; neither did Lily Tindale, which struck her mother and father as curious, although not particularly alarming. When the meal was over and his daughter still had not turned up, John Tindale went looking for her. He recalled seeing her enter the stack yard and thought that this might be the best place to begin his search. He called his daughter's name and began poking around the bales of straw. Tindale's foot caught against something which was laying, concealed by a mass of loose straw. When he investigated, he found that it was his daughter's body.

For any parent to stumble across the corpse of their child would be a distressing experience, but for John Tindale, the horror was beyond all imagining. Not only was his daughter dead, she had died in the most hideous manner possible, by having her throat cut so savagely that only her spinal cord had prevented her from being completely decapitated. Both the straw and the child's clothes were saturated with blood. As if this was not bad enough, the girl's face was also battered and bruised. She had been the subject of the most brutal attack. Although the autopsy revealed that she had not been raped, he clothing was disarranged, as though an attempt had been made to assault her sexually.

It did not take the dead girl's father long to connect the fact that his daughter had not come for her meal and neither had one of the workers. John Thompson was nowhere to be seen and none of the other men had seen him since about 1:00 pm. When he went to Molescroft to report the violent death of his daughter to the police, John Tindale told them of his suspicions about the shepherd.

When they came to examine Lily Tindale's body, the officers found something interesting and quite possibly significant. Laying on her chest was a plug of tobacco. The importance of this discovery only became clear when a police officer who had walked to the village of Molescroft, half a mile from Constitution Hill Farm, to enquire if anybody had seen the missing shepherd, returned with the news that he had visited the Molescroft Inn at midday to purchase some tobacco. The inference was plain, that Thompson had killed the child and perhaps spilled or dropped some of his tobacco on her in the struggle.

It was 6:00 pm before Sergeant Jackson of the Beverley police spotted John Thompson, who was known to him. Suspicions against Thompson could only be intensified by the fact that when apprehended, it was found that his clothes were heavily stained with blood; as were the contents of his pockets. Specifically, a clasp knife and pipe were found to be smeared with blood. When asked to account for his gory appearance, Thompson claimed to have been bleeding a sheep, a traditional remedy in those days for some illnesses among livestock.

Once John Thompson was in custody, things moved rapidly. It was established that the blood on his clothes was in fact human, although the tests used a century ago were not sensitive enough to be able to give the exact group. But the fact that the man's clothes were soaked with human blood and that he had lied about this when questioned, certainly indicated that he had something to hide. The clasp knife which was found in his pocket when he was arrested was not nearly sharp enough to have caused such a fearful wound to the dead child's neck and so the police began questioning their suspect closely. Thompson soon admitted that earlier that day, he had had in his possession not only the knife, but also an open razor. Part of the statement which he made to the police when being questioned, consisted of the following passage:

The knife found in my pocket which has bloodstains on it was done bleeding a sheep. I put the razor down a hedgerow as I went down the Leconfield Road.

After retracing the route which Thompson claimed to have taken and managing to identify his boot marks in the mud of the lane, the police succeeded in finding the hedgerow where he had said that he dropped the razor. It was laying where Thompson had said it would be. With the razor was part of the case in which it was usually kept. The other part was later found beneath Lily Tindale's body. The pieces of the case against Thompson all seemed to be fitting together perfectly.

Things then moved with dizzying speed. John Thompson had been arrested on 15 February. After the inquest on Lily Tindale had named Thompson as her murderer, he was remanded for trial at the next assizes in York, which were due to begin on 9 March. In other words, the accused man found himself standing in the dock and facing trial a little over three weeks after his arrest. So overwhelming was the evidence against the man accused of this horrible crime, that the trial was very brief. There could be not the slightest doubt that John Thompson had beaten young Lily around the face and then nearly severed her head from her body. The only thing lacking was a motive.

The razor with which John Thompson had cut Lily Tindale's throat was his own and was normally to be found on the mantelpiece of his rented room. Obviously, he had put it in his pocket before setting out to work that fateful day. If he merely wished to threaten the girl, then surely his clasp knife would have done just as well as the razor. That the dead girl's skirt was raised and her underclothes disordered, hinted that Thompson had some carnal motive in attacking her; but if so, why on earth cut her throat with such ferocity? It is unlikely that we shall ever learn the true motive for the murder. What is beyond doubt is that it was actually John Thompson who killed the child. While he was in the condemned cell and awaiting execution, Thompson was visited regularly by the Wesleyan chaplain. Shortly before he was hanged, Thompson confessed to the chaplain that he was guilty and that the verdict was a just one.

On 27 March 1917, John Thompson was hanged in Leeds's Armley Prison. The executioner was Thomas Pierrepoint. The whole process, from committing the murder to the appointment with the hangman had taken just forty days, which set a twentieth-century record for speedy executions.

Thomas Cox: A Present for his Son

Hanged at Shrewsbury, 19 December 1917

Tolstoy remarks in the opening paragraph of *Anna Karenina* that all happy families are happy in the same way, but that unhappy families are each unhappy in their own particular way. The distinctive way in which the Cox family of Ludlow were unhappy was that the husband and wife regularly fought like cat and dog in front of their children. Henry Cox was 13 years old and did his best to protect his 8-year-old brother Benjamin from the worst of the unpleasantness; but this was not always possible. The friction between 59-year-old Thomas Cox and his wife Elizabeth was more or less incessant. Matters were not perhaps helped by the fact that their accommodation at 37 Upper Galdeford was cramped in the extreme. In fact the entire family slept in one bedroom. This meant that, inevitably, their two sons were privy to every aspect of their parents' disputes.

On 9 August 1917, the whole family went out to collect firewood. Coal was expensive, but sticks and branches picked up from common land were free and the Cox family were always short of money. The day passed without any major incident between Cox and his wife. The following day, a Friday, it was business as usual, with husband and wife squabbling continuously, all day long. The arguments raged well into the night, with Thomas Cox accusing his wife of spreading lies about him throughout the town of Ludlow. At about 2:30 am on the morning of Saturday, 11 August, young Henry was awoken by more shouting. He heard his father ask rhetorically of his wife, 'What do you want to tell so many lies about me for?' There was a pause and then Henry Cox heard his mother scream loudly as she was struck in the face by her husband. Thomas Cox then jumped from the bed and left the room.

Mrs Cox lit a lamp and asked Henry to fetch a bowl of water, as the blow her husband had given her had injured her head. Her son left the room and filled a bowl with water. While he was doing so, he heard his mother screaming again and he stopped what he was doing and ran back to the bedroom. As he approached it, he heard his mother saying, 'Don't, for the sake of the children!' When he entered the bedroom, he saw that his mother was laying on the floor and that his father was standing over her with something shiny in his hand. To Henry's horror, he saw that there was a great quantity of blood splashed down the front of his mother's nightdress and he asked her, 'Has he cut your throat?' His mother replied that this was indeed the case.

Turning to his father, the boy asked him why he had done such a dreadful thing. Thomas Cox said, 'She should not tell so many lies about me. She is canting all over the town about me.' Young Henry asked whether he should go to fetch his aunt, who lived nearby, but his father told him to go back to sleep. Frightened out of his wits, the boy endeavoured to do as he was told and, after extinguishing the lamp, went back to bed.

At 7:20 the following morning, young Henry was woken by his father, who told him to go to one of the neighbours and raise the alarm. Henry was horrified to observe that his father too had his throat cut. Once again, we see the familiar motif of the man who murders his wife by cutting her throat with a razor and then attempts to end his own life in the same way. Thomas Cox had seemingly made a more determined effort than those husbands at whom we looked earlier. He had lost a considerable amount of blood by the time that he sent his son for help.

Instead of going to a neighbour, Henry Cox ran to his aunt's house, which was a few streets away. Mary Ward lived at 30 Old Street and when she heard what her nephew had to tell her, she sent at once for the police. Accompanied by police constable Charles Morris, she and her nephew went to the scene of the tragedy. All that Thomas Cox was able to say was that he had no idea at all why he had done it.

The trial of Thomas Cox was held at the Shrewsbury Assizes on 8 November that same year, before Mr Justice Atkin. Cox's defence counsel made the best of a bad job, by pleading that his client had suffered from a fit of temporary insanity. The evidence was very much against this claim. Mr Cotes-Preedy, for the prosecution, pointed out that there was every indication that this murder had been premeditated and not the sudden and impulsive act that the defence was anxious that it should appear. There was, for instance, the undeniable fact that Thomas Cox was bearded and never shaved. Yet he had killed his wife with an open razor for which he could have had no possible use. The explanation advanced for this was far from convincing. Thomas Cox's eldest son, also called Thomas, was fighting in France and was due home on leave. Cox had supposedly bought the razor a day or two before the murder, intending it to be a present for his son.

One fact which weighed heavily against Thomas Cox was that, just like Charles Frembd three years earlier, he had attacked his wife with a razor and killed her while she lay defenceless in bed. This looked like a ruthless murder, without even the feeble excuse that it had taken place in the course of a physical fight. Indeed, Henry Cox was able to state clearly that his mother had not made any aggressive moves against her husband.

Counsel for the defence mentioned that Cox had attempted to kill himself on a previous occasion, but since this had been some years before the murder, this was dismissed as being irrelevant to the case. The suggestion of the prosecution, which was accepted by the jury, was that Thomas Cox had decided to kill his wife and had bought an open razor with the express purpose of cutting her throat while she lay helplessly in bed. The jury took little time in deliberating before bring in a verdict of 'guilty'; following which Mr Justice Atkin passed sentence of death.

The defence applied for leave to appeal and Thomas Cox's appeal was heard in London, a month later before Mr Justice Darling. The main thrust of the defence was that the trial judge had been wrong to dismiss the significance of the earlier suicide attempt and that this cast light upon Cox's mental state and indicated that he was unbalanced and prone to irrational actions. It did not take the Court of Criminal Appeal long to deal with the case and announce that there was no reason for them to interfere with the verdict. On 19 December, Thomas Cox was hanged at Shrewsbury prison by John Ellis.

Chapter Two

Butchers at Work: Two Axe Murderers

In the last chapter, we looked at one type of murder which has fallen from fashion, due in large part to the decline in ready availability of open razors in the average modern home. Another murder weapon which is seldom seen lying around people's houses these days, at least in this country, is the axe. The decline of the axe murder is also a consequence of changing lifestyles. In the days before central heating, when almost every home had fireplaces where coal was burned, it was necessary to maintain a regular supply of kindling. Coal must be heated steadily before it will catch fire and for this purpose, a blaze must first be started with paper and wood. Once this is going merrily, the coal will then begin to burn. At one time, every corner shop sold bundles of kindling wood for this purpose; logs split into thin pieces. For many, this was a needless extravagance though and most working- class households contained a hatchet, a short handled axe. This was used to break large pieces of wood into the smaller splinters and short portions useful for kindling a coal fire.

It was these compact, short-handled axes which were at one time popular for use in domestic murders. They were often to be found lying around the kitchen and were just the right size for launching a deadly assault in a confined space. The fact that they could be swung with one hand made them the ideal weapon for those murderers who were not especially squeamish; the axe murder being a notoriously bloody affair.

There were of course disadvantages in using an axe to rid one's self of an annoying wife or troublesome family. Chief of these in the days when murder carried the death penalty was that it was almost unheard of for an axe murderer to be reprieved by the Home Secretary. Those killers who mutilate their victims either before or after death have always been viewed with extreme disfavour by the British judicial system.

Two famous axe murders took place during the First World War. One of these was the so-called Wallasey Hatchet Murders. We shall look first though at a somewhat less well-known case, that of Joseph Deans who, in October 1916, murdered the woman he loved with an axe and then attempted suicide by cutting his own throat with a razor.

Joseph Deans: An Axe for the Lady

Hanged at Durham, 20 December 1916

If ever a man signalled his clear intention of committing murder, then that man was Joseph Deans. Before actually killing his victim, he had threatened her with a knife, attempted to strangle her, tried to buy a gun to kill her and told all his friends at various times what his intentions were towards the woman he would eventually hack to death with an axe. Just as there are those who are constantly threatening or supposedly attempting suicide, although never succeeding in their apparent aim, so too there are people who talk too often of murder. After a while, the hearers will dismiss such lurid claims and tell each other that they have heard it all before. This can be a mistake, because the habitual threatener of suicide or murder will, from time to time, fulfil their promises.

After spending twenty years in South Africa, first as a soldier and then as a gold miner, 44-year-old Joseph Deans returned to his native country in 1913 and settled once more in Sunderland, the town in north-east England where he had grown up. He was, for the time, a well-to-do man, with a pension of over £2 a week from the South African Government, as well as a fair sum of money to show for all his years of prospecting and mining. Two years after returning to Britain, Deans picked up with a widow with two daughters. Her name was Catherine Convery and it was not long before Deans was absolutely infatuated with her. He gave all his attention and considerable amounts of his money to the widow; who, by all accounts, did not return his affections as whole-heartedly as he might have wished. Indeed, it was Deans' contention that Catherine Convery was two-timing him. He complained that after he had lavished a good deal of love and much of his money on her, she had begun carrying on with another man.

There were fearful rows between Joseph Deans and his paramour, often accompanied by the use or threat of violence. On one occasion, for example, Deans struck his girlfriend in the presence of her daughter; accusing her of being unfaithful to him. Having knocked her to the floor, he snatched up a knife, saying, 'I will do it now!' The daughter understood this to mean that Deans was about to murder her mother. She ran to protect her mother, whereupon Deans put down the knife and left the house, but not before declaring to Catherine Convery, 'I haven't long to live, but before I die I'll kill you!'

Some days later, neighbours observed Mrs Convery running down the street, pursued by Joseph Deans. In his hand was a length of rope. The terrified woman told onlookers, 'He's going to choke me!'

On Tuesday, 3 October 1916, Joseph Deans went into a gun shop in Monkwearmouth, the district of Sunderland in which he lived, and tried to buy a revolver. Although he had already acquired a firearms certificate which entitled him to own a pistol, the owner of the shop, Mr Garrick, declined to sell him the gun he wanted, because when examining the weapon, Deans had asked, 'Will it kill a man?'

Over the course of the next few days, Joseph Dean began giving away his belongings to various friends and acquaintances. This kind of behaviour can sometimes be the precursor to suicide, but it seemed to have aroused no apprehensions in Deans' social circle. He gave the appearance of a man putting his affairs in order, repaying trifling sums of money that he owed and so on. On the afternoon of Saturday, 7 October Joseph Dean met an old friend called Thomas Thompson and gave him a watch and chain and two gold rings as presents. He also showed this man a photograph of Catherine Convery and told him, 'I love every hair of her head, but I'm going to finish her off tonight.'

Later that same day, Deans went to an ironmonger's shop and bought a small axe, which he asked to be wrapped up in brown paper. He then went to see a man called John Donkin, to whom he owed a few shillings. After paying Donkin the money, Deans showed him an open razor and said, 'The axe is for the lady, the razor's for myself.' After this encounter, Joseph Deans visited the Grey Horse pub in Howard Street, where he spent the rest of the afternoon, not leaving until 7:00 pm.

At about 7:30 pm, Catherine Convery staggered into the Grey Horse, clutching at a gaping wound in her neck and crying, 'He's murdered me this time!' At about the same time that Mrs Convery entered the pub, streaming with blood, Joseph Deans went into the yard at the back of the Grey Horse and cut his own throat. The wound was not deep though and he was arrested and charged with the attempted murder of Catherine Convery. The injured woman lingered on in hospital for six days before dying. This was truly remarkable, in light of the severity of her wounds. In addition to the cut on her neck, Mrs Convery had a wound to her shoulder and, most seriously of all, a gash across the top of her head which had shattered the skull and exposed her brain to view. It was this injury which, in the opinion of the doctors tending her, proved fatal. When he was charged with murder, Deans said, 'It's all that woman. She's had hundreds of pounds off me and wanted to toss me away now.

There could be no real doubt about where responsibility lay for Catherine Convery's death and the at his trial before Judge Low at Durham Assizes on 15 November, the jury took only five minutes to convict him of murder. His defence had been one of temporary insanity, but the meticulous preparations made for the murder and the fact that he had telegraphed his intentions over several weeks made this improbable. After sentence of death had been passed, Deans said, 'I killed the woman and I'm pleased I killed her.'; words which were to come back to haunt him when a few weeks later, his appeal against the conviction was heard at the Royal Courts of Justice in London.

During his appeal, Deans was lodged in Pentonville Prison, where the food was apparently far better than that to which he was used in Durham. It did not take long to dismiss the appeal, it being pointed out to the prisoner that he had admitted in open court at his trial that he had committed murder and was glad about it.

Joseph Deans's execution which, in the event, did not run at all smoothly, was scheduled for 20 December 1916. His stay in Durham prison when he returned from the unsuccessful appeal hearing in London was marked by a curious incident. So used had the condemned man to being fed well while he was staying in Pentonville, that on his return to Durham he began to complain about the quality of the food being provided for him there.

When Deans first objected to the food at Durham, he was told by the warders that it was wartime and he would just have to take what was offered. He insisted on seeing the prison doctor who, on hearing about the diet which had been provided in London, decided that as Joseph Deans only had a few weeks to live, it would be kind at least to make his meals the best that the prison could manage. From then on, he had bacon for breakfast and various other luxuries denied to the average prisoner.

One of the things that had been worrying John Ellis, the executioner, for some time was the number of condemned men who had attempted suicide by cutting their throats. Dropping somebody with a wound on their neck, six feet and allowing them to come to a neck-breaking jerk at the end of the drop can be a chancy business. On more than one occasion, wounds had opened during hangings, but not to any great extent. Ellis was concerned though that one day there would be a catastrophe and that in a worst case scenario, with a severe injury to the neck, he might even end up tearing somebody's head off entirely; something which actually happened during several nineteenth century hangings. So it was that during Joseph Dean's execution, Ellis planned to place the knot in a different position; thus minimising the risk of opening up the wound in his throat. As we shall see, this did not prove possible.

Even before his decision to alter the method of hanging Deans, a slight difficulty had arisen about the execution. In order to operate the trapdoors on which the prisoner stood, a long lever had to be operated. To prevent the trapdoors being opened accidentally, a split pin was used to hold the lever in place. This needed to be removed before the lever could be pulled. Ellis found that the pin was very stiff and that he might have difficulty pulling it out before using the lever during the execution. He asked the prison engineer if he would help on the day of the hanging, by pulling the pin out when Ellis was about to operate the lever, but the man refused to take any part in an execution. The executioner replaced the stiff pin with a thinner piece of metal, but it was one more unusual feature of an execution in which nothing seemed destined to go right.

The execution of Joseph Deans turned out to be one of the most confused and disorganised that Ellis had ever known. Pinioning the prisoner in his cell went smoothly enough and, leaving the condemned man in charge of his assistant, Ellis walked briskly off to the scaffold, in order to be waiting there with the hood when his assistant escorted the prisoner to the gallows. A few seconds after leaving the cell, the executioner was taken aback to hear the clatter of running footsteps coming up behind him. He turned round and was astonished to see that so eager was Deans to have the execution over and done with, that he was literally running to his death. Ellis's assistant, George Brown, was having to run to keep up with the man who was to be hanged that morning.

It struck Ellis that this was likely to be one of the swiftest executions of his career. That was until the chaplain, who had arranged to meeting the little procession to the gallows as it entered the execution shed, turned up and blocked Deans's headlong rush. The old minister put his hand on the doomed man's shoulder and told him, 'Take your time.' Because the chaplain was very old and incapable of moving at any great speed, the party moving towards the gallows suddenly slowed down to a snail's pace, as the old man recited the burial service for the dead.

This unexpected change of pace was disconcerting to John Ellis and he moved on ahead to wait at the noose, ready to place the hood over Deans's head and the rope around his neck. It was at this point that what should have been a most solemn business descended into farce.

Once Joseph Deans was standing on the trapdoors, all that was necessary was for the executioner himself to pull the hood over the condemned man's head and adjust the rope around his neck. While this was being done, the assistant would be buckling a strap around the prisoner's ankles, fastening it at the back. In the event, as soon as Ellis had arranged the hood over his head, Deans immediately turned round until he faced the opposite way. Why he should have done so, nobody ever knew. The sudden movement threw Ellis out of his stride though and he forgot about his idea for positioning the knot in a different part of the man's neck, in order to avoid the self-inflicted wound on his throat. Meanwhile, George Brown, the assistant executioner, had jumped up and moved round, so that he could buckle Deans' ankles from behind, as was the custom.

John Ellis, becoming a little flustered, now took the hooded man's shoulders and turned him round again so that he was facing the executioner. As he fastened the noose, Ellis was aware that his assistant had had to jump up again, so that he could once more move around Deans and get behind him to fasten his legs from the rear. At this point, Ellis felt that there had been enough delays and, fearful that if they waited any longer then the condemned man might faint, as not uncommonly happened during an execution, ordered the assistant off the scaffold, before the man had had a chance to strap Deans's ankles together. The drop fell with Joseph Deans legs not secured together.

The execution of Joseph Deans left Ellis feeling very harassed and confused. He preferred hangings to go smoothly, without any fuss and bother. The next time that he hanged an axe murderer, the execution was a textbook example of how such operations should be conducted, with no hitches or unpleasantness of any sort. The only point of note was that the man he hanged on that occasion, William Hodgson, may very well have been innocent.

William Hodgson: The Wallasey Hatchet Murders

Hanged at Liverpool, 16 August 1917

Few crimes excite more horror and disgust than the murder of a small child. When the killing of a child is undertaken with an axe, then the revulsion felt by ordinary people is liable to be magnified a hundred-fold and those who end up in the dock for such brutal crimes may expect little mercy from the courts.

In August 1916 Eleanor Yates Law and her husband William were living at No 14 Central Park Avenue, in the Wallasey district of Liverpool. That month, new neighbours moved into the semi-detached house which adjoined that of the Laws. The Hodgsons, who arrived to take possession of No 16, seemed a pleasant and unremarkable family, consisting of 33-year-old William Hodgson, his wife Margaret, who was 36, and her 3-year-old daughter, who was also called Margaret. There was also a baby, only a few months old, by the name of Cyril. William Hodgson worked as a buyer for Robb Brothers, a drapers shop in Birkenhead. All in all, a perfectly normal and respectable, lower middle-class family.

In the eight months following the Hodgson family moving in to No 16, the Laws found their neighbours to be friendly enough. They often heard the sound of arguments between Mr and Mrs Hodgson, but then all couples row from time to time. The Laws' daughter played with little Margaret Hodgson and neither the Laws nor anybody else found anything out of the ordinary about the Hodgson family.

Over the winter of 1916, a most unpleasant criminal haunted Liverpool. The man tricked his way into homes when the husband was out at work and then threatened lone women with a hatchet, before sexually assaulting them and stealing various items from their homes. These attacks continued until the spring of 1917.

On the morning of Monday, 16 April 1917, Mrs Laws was in her kitchen at about 7:40 am, when she heard the little girl next door say clearly, 'Don't do that.' She thought that the child's voice came from the scullery of No 16. The child did not sound frightened or alarmed and she heard nothing more until there was the sound of a man's footsteps in the backyard of No 16. She assumed this to be Mr Hodgson getting ready to leave the house to go to work.

We are able to piece together William Hodgson's movements that day. He went to work at the draper's shop as usual and nobody noticed anything untoward. After work, he went for a drink with another employee, not returning home until 7:30 that evening. This was not unusual. Some of the quarrels between Hodgson and his wife related to his fondness for visiting the pub in the evening, rather than staying home with his wife and children.

Throughout the day, Mrs Law thought that next door's baby, Cyril, was crying a lot. By evening, she began to think that something might be wrong, because nobody appeared to be attending to the child. At 6:00 pm, she went next door and knocked on the front door. This was unlocked and she called out before entering the house. The baby was still crying, although she didn't know where in the house it was. When she entered the scullery, Mrs Law received the shock of her life, because she saw the body of Mrs Margaret Hodgson. It was laying on the floor, covered in blood.

When the police were called, it was found that not only was William Hodgson's wife dead, so was his 3-year-old daughter. There was no mystery about how they had died, because a blood-spattered hatchet lay on the floor by the bodies. There was blood all over the kitchen. As well as blood, brain tissue too had been splashed over the floor and walls. The place looked like a slaughterhouse; it had clearly been a frenzied killing. On the kitchen table were an empty purse and money box and in the front room was a suitcase, which had been packed with various valuable items from the house. It looked as though the serial sex attacker haunting Liverpool had now progressed to murder.

When William Hodgson returned home, he was told by the police of the death of his wife and daughter. The baby, who had been found upstairs, was unharmed. Hodgson told the police that neither the suitcase nor the hatchet used in the murders were his. Indeed, he showed them where he kept his own small axe for chopping firewood. He was taken to the police station to make a statement and then allowed to return home. Later that same day though, he was arrested and charged with the murder of his wife and daughter.

Friends, neighbours and workmates were astounded to hear that William Hodgson stood accused of such a brutal crime. Surely, the police must have made a terrible mistake? Hodgson was an assistant in a draper's shop, with no history of violence and nothing out of the ordinary about his life. Why on earth would he have hacked his family to death with an axe? The revelations which gradually came out about William Hodgson's private life gave a possible motive, as well as causing the whole country to take a salacious interest in the case.

For a year, William Hodgson had been conducting an intense love affair with a waitress at the café in Birkenhead where he ate his lunch during the week. This young woman, Eleanor Llewellyn, believed Hodgson to be single and had no idea at all that he was married and lived with his family. Soon after taking her to the cinema and for a meal, Hodgson suggested to Eleanor that they begin visiting a hotel which rented rooms by the hour for just such liasons as he had in mind.

For almost a year, William Hodgson led a double life, as the boyfriend of the young waitress and also as the head of a family. Then disaster struck. On 21 March 1917, Eleanor Llewellyn announced to her mother that she was pregnant. A hundred years ago, an illegitimate baby was the ruination of a woman and her mother immediately set out to save her daughter from disgrace. The most obvious way of achieving this end would of course be for the father of Eleanor's unborn child to make an honest woman of her by marriage. This was a perfectly reasonable solution to the situation and neither Eleanor nor her mother could understand Hodgson's apparent reluctance to do the honourable thing. They were not of course to know that there was an insurmountable obstacle to his marrying anybody.

Over the next few weeks, Hodgson wrote a number of letters to Eleanor Llewellyn, which she and her mother interpreted as being proposals of marriage. One said, for example:

> *If you have the patience to wait until after Easter, we will make some arrangements, so don't worry, it will be all right. We will meet before long, and I think we shall both be satisfied and your mother too.*

Not unnaturally, given the circumstances, both Eleanor Llewellyn and her mother took this to mean that William Hodgson was prepared to get married after Easter.

Wanting to make sure that Hodgson was going to stand by this pledge, Mrs Llewellyn visited Robb Brothers, the shop where William Hodgson was working, on the very morning of the murder, in order to press her prospective son-in-law about his intentions. Although his behaviour that day was more or less normal, a fellow employee said that he had become agitated after the visit of Mrs Llewellyn.

Once the police knew about Hodgson's clandestine affair with the waitress and of her pregnancy, they thought that they had found the perfect motive for murder; the only difficulty being that the actual evidence against their prime suspect was decidedly thin. The indications were that Mrs Hodgson and her daughter, 3-year-old Margaret, had been killed between eight and ten in the morning. There was no food in their stomachs, which suggested that they had died before having a chance to eat breakfast. A lot hinged upon the time that William Hodgson had left the house that day. He claimed that he had been on his way to work by 8:35 am and there was no evidence to contradict this time. If he had murdered his wife and daughter, then he must have walked out of the front door almost immediately afterwards. And yet nobody noticed anything the least bit out of the ordinary about him that day. It would take a peculiarly cold blooded man to slaughter his family in so grisly a fashion before breakfast and then spend a normal day at work.

One very significant point was that the kitchen was quite literally awash with blood and liberally splashed with brain matter. Both victims had had their heads smashed in with the axe and blood had flown up the walls during the murder. One might imagine that the killer himself would be covered in blood after such exertions. Sir Bernard Spilsbury, the famous pathologist, examined the clothes that Hodgson had been wearing that day and found a number of minute spots of blood. There were some on the outside of the trouser legs, a half dozen almost invisible specks on the front of the waistcoat and two tiny stains on the left boot, but none at all on the right. One curious point was that Sir Bernard thought that all these flecks of blood had clotted *before* landing on the clothing. In other words, this was not blood which had been flying about when the murders were being committed, but had got on the clothing after they had almost dried.

William Hodgson's trial for murder began before Mr Justice Avory at the Chester Assizes on 13 July 1917. The thrust of the prosecution case was concerned more with proving that Hodgson *could* have committed the murder and that he had a powerful motive for doing so, rather than in demonstrating that he *had* murdered his wife and daughter. The evidence was, after all, purely circumstantial. Neighbours were called to give evidence about the arguments that he and his wife had had, witnesses said that Hodgson had a vicious temper and had struck his little daughter on the back once, it was shown that he was an adulterer. None of this was sufficient to prove that William Hodgson had laid about his family with a hatchet on that fateful April morning. The most that could be said was that it would not have been impossible.

Despite the weakness of the prosecution case, the jury took just 14 minutes to find Hodgson guilty of the murders and he was duly sentenced to death. There was an appeal, which was dismissed almost contemptuously. On 16 August, Hodgson was hanged at Liverpool's Walton prison by John Ellis. The executioner entered the condemned cell at 9:00 am and Hodgson was dead within 30 seconds. There was something about William Hodgson which seemed to capture the attention of women; even strangers. On the morning of his execution, a crowd consisting mainly of young women gathered outside the prison to hear the tolling of the bell which told them that the hanging had taken place. Because there was very little to write about after the execution had taken place, one newspaper drew attention to what it claimed was an extraordinary coincidence associated with the case; namely that Hodgson lived at house No 16, committed his crime on the 16th of one month and was hanged on the 16th of another.

There exists the very real possibility that Hodgson was innocent of the crime for which he was hanged. It is all but unbelievable that in the course of a frenzied attack that saw blood and brains flying up the walls, the killer should not himself have been liberally splattered with gore. The fact that the tiny specks of blood found on Hodgson's clothes had been almost dry when they came into contact with the cloth, suggested that he picked them up when he returned home after the murder and helped the police by, for example, opening a kitchen cupboard to show them where he kept his own hatchet. The story of his adultery and causing the pregnancy of the young waitress told heavily against him in court and such heartless philandering could not fail to have prejudiced the jury against him. Perhaps the best verdict would have been that which is available to Scottish, but not English, juries. North of the border, it is possible to dodge the question of innocence or guilt entirely, by returning a verdict of 'Not Proven'. This means, in effect, that while strong suspicion attaches itself to the defendant, the evidence falls far short of being conclusive.

Chapter Three

Another Old Fashioned Murder Weapon:
The Domestic Poker

We have in the last two chapters looked at two murder weapons which have fallen into disuse. Readers may rack their brains in vain to recall the last time they read in the newspapers of anybody in this country being despatched with a razor or hatchet! This is, as we have seen, because these implements are no longer to be found laying around casually in the average home. There is another tool which was also exceedingly popular at one time with domestic murderers and this too has been out of favour with killers for many years. Let us look at a quotation from that most popular of Charles Dickens's books, *David Copperfield*. Betsy Trotwood is expressing her irritation at hearing of the marriage of David's childhood nurse:

> *'I only hope,' said my aunt, shaking her head, 'That her husband is one of these Poker husbands who abound in the newspapers and will beat her well with one.'*

Modern readers might perhaps be left scratching their heads and wondering what on earth a 'Poker husband' might be.

For those who have grown up without living in a house warmed by open fires, a poker is a long steel rod with one pointed end and often an ornamental knob at the other end. It was, as its name suggests, used for poking dying fires and rekindling their vigour by moving unburned chunks of wood and coal into the heart of the blaze. Laying as they did by the hearthside, the poker was often the first thing which came to hand when somebody was casting around for a weapon. Violent men would beat their wives with the poker, often causing the most terrible injuries and even, as we shall see in the next case, bring about their deaths.

One of the problems with the poker is that because one end was sharp, it could, in addition to being used for striking somebody with the side of the rod, be used like a sword and jabbed into the face or skull. Figure 3 shows an illustration of just such a crime, with the poker sticking out of an abused wife's head. In the first such case at which we are looking, even more fearful injuries than this were caused to a woman when her husband snatched up the poker and set about her. This murder is of interest because it was one of the few cases when executioner John Ellis knew the man he was to hang.

James Hargreaves: 'Big Jim' Wields a Poker

Hanged at Manchester, 19 December 1916
One of the things which readers might by now have noticed from the murders at which we have been looking, is that human nature does not appear to have changed greatly over the last century. Men and women were drinking to excess, hopping in and out of other people's beds and generally carrying on much as they do today. Then, as now, there was a strong and direct association between the excessive consumption of alcohol and levels of domestic violence.

In 1914, 38-year-old Caroline McGhee grew tired of her husband and returned to her mother's home in Ashton-under-Lyne. After a while, her mother had had enough of this arrangement, because her daughter was a heavy drinker, who was apt to get into trouble when she had too much to drink. It was about this time that Caroline met up with 54-year-old James Hargreaves, who was known to everybody as 'Big Jim'. It was an apt enough nickname, because although he was only five-and-a-half feet tall, Hargreaves weighed fourteen stone. He had a reputation too for being quite handy with his fists.

After a few months, Hargreaves too became tired of his new girlfriend's drunkenness and he asked her to leave. She then moved into her brother Oscar's home. He too found her drinking more than he could tolerate and so after three months, she moved back with Hargreaves at 9 Orange Street in Ashton-under-Lyne. Things went smoothly enough for a while, until the summer of 1916.

On 7 August 1916, Caroline McGhee went out drinking with an old friend of hers called Lily Armitage; and by the end of the evening they were so drunk that Caroline slept at her friend's house. The next day, they bumped into Big Jim Hargreaves, who did not seem unduly concerned at hearing that his girlfriend had stayed the night at Lily Armitage's place. It had happened before and he seemingly accepted these occasional absences as the price to be paid for living with a woman who was, to say the least, fond of a drink. The three of them then went to the nearest pub and starting drinking. By the early evening, Hargreaves had had enough and announced that he was going home to have something to eat.

Caroline and Lily went on to another public house called the Commercial Hotel. They met up with two soldiers by the name of Edward Uttley and William Sumner and accepted the men's offer of buying them drinks. It is hard to avoid the suspicion that these soldiers thought that they were onto a good thing and that their generosity might result in some romantic liaison with the women upon whom they were lavishing their money and attention. At any rate, the four of them continued drinking, moving on at one point to another pub called the Nelson and then returning to the Commercial Hotel. At eleven that night, Caroline McGhee set in train the sequence of events which would ultimately cost her her life. She invited her friend Lily and the two soldiers to come to the house she was sharing with James Hargreaves, telling them that there was a bottle of whisky there.

Surprisingly enough, Big Jim didn't appear in the least put out when his girlfriend rolled up with three other people, seemingly intent upon drinking his whisky. He even went out and bought some tripe and then cooked it for them, while they drank the whiskey. After half an hour, Lily Armitage left with one of the soldiers and the remaining soldier left a short while later, parting on good terms with Hargreaves. It looked as though the evening had gone off smoothly.

The next day, Wednesday, 9 August, James Hargreaves was in Katherine Street, not far from his home. He saw a police officer whom he knew well, Detective Constable Robert Wilson. He went up to him and said, 'Oh Bob, what must I do? I've murdered a woman at our house last night. I hit her on the head with a poker.' Wilson advised his friend to say no more and arrested him. At the police station, Hargreaves was cautioned again by

Sergeant Henry Gregson. On being cautioned, Big Jim Hargreaves made the following statement:

> *She came home drunk and had a bottle of whiskey. We had it between us and she threw the bottle at me. I caught it. She said she was the missus there. One thing brought on another. She threw the bottle at me and smashed me in the face. She hit me again, so I hit her with the poker and her number was up.*

After such a confession, it is little wonder that the police locked Hargreaves in a cell and went to his house to see what had happened.

In the bedroom at 9 Orange Street, DC Robert Wilson and Sergeant Gregson found a scene of horror. Caroline McGhee was laying on the bed. She was covered in blood and there was a large pool of blood beneath the bed as well. Blood had been splashed all over the place; flecks were found on the curtains and even on the ceiling. A cursory examination of the room revealed the extraordinary ferocity of the attack to which the dead woman had been subjected. In the hearth were Caroline's false teeth, which were covered in blood. There was something even worse. Laying in the cinders, next to the false teeth, were two pieces of Caroline's skull. The attack with the poker had shattered her head quite literally to pieces.

On 11 August, just two days after Hargreaves had been arrested, an inquest named him as the killer of Caroline McGhee and he was remanded for trial at the next assizes, which were held on 28 November 1916, before Mr Justice Avory. There was no question that James Hargreaves had beaten his girlfriend to death with a poker and the only faint hope for the man in the dock was that he might be convicted of manslaughter rather than murder, thus escaping the gallows.

Dr Donald Falconer had examined the scene of the killing and his evidence to the court was grim. He said that Caroline McGhee's skull had been, 'shattered to atoms' by many blows. Her brain was exposed and fragments of bone from her skull were scattered about the room. The poker itself was covered in blood, hair and brain tissue.

Big Jim's defence was that he had objected to the soldiers being brought to the house and that there had been a violent row about this. He claimed that he had really acted in self defence, because Caroline had struck the first blow at him with the empty whiskey bottle. Those in court looked at the powerfully-built, tough-looking man in the dock and tried to imagine him fearing for his life because a drunken, middle-aged woman had thrown a bottle at him. It was an implausible enough scenario and not one that the jury felt inclined to accept. After Hargreaves was found guilty, Mr Justice Avory donned the black cap and passed sentence of death. There was no appeal and the execution was fixed for Tuesday, 19 December 1916.

As was the custom, John Ellis arrived at Strangeways prison in Manchester on the afternoon before the execution. In order to calculate the most efficacious drop to give the condemned man, Ellis had to see the man in person, so that he could assess the thickness of the neck muscles and so on. The thought that he might be being sized-up by the hangman would be an unnerving experience for anybody and to spare his victim this, it was John Ellis's habit to put on a prison warder's uniform and then observe the man while wearing this. Hargreaves was being take to be weighed and so Ellis simply lingered in the corridor to watch him as he passed.

When Big Jim Hargreaves came into sight along the gas-lit corridor, John Ellis almost gasped out loud, because he realised that he knew the man. Although he had never learned his surname, Hargreaves, like Ellis was a dog-racing enthusiast and they had often chatted together at races in Lancashire. Ellis said later that he had never had a greater shock during his professional business as a hangman, as that which he received when he found that he knew the man whom he was to hang the next day.

A curious circumstance, and one which runs counter to all our intuitive assumptions, is that men under sentence of death very often put on a lot of weight while waiting to be executed. One might have thought that the prospect of being hanged might take away one's appetite, but this was not the case. James Hargreaves, for example, had gained an astonishing 15 pounds in the three weeks since he had been convicted. Taking into account the man's age, 54, and his weight and height, Ellis decided that a fairly modest drop of five feet and four inches would be sufficient.

On the morning of the execution, John Ellis was struck by the change in the man that he had known so well. Hargreaves, not surprisingly, gave the impression of a man in the grip of a deep depression. The arrangement in Strangeways was that the scaffold was right next door to the condemned cell. At a previous execution there, somebody had timed how long the whole process took and found that from leaving the cell until the man was dangling at the end of the rope, had taken only eight seconds. This was however under the ideal circumstances of a man who walked briskly and willingly to his death. This was not how it was to be with James Hargreaves.

When he entered the condemned cell, it was plain to John Ellis that the man he was to hang could barely move, so paralysed was he with fear. After strapping Hargreaves's hands behind his back, Ellis led the doomed man to the scaffold. That short distance took almost a minute to cover, which was five times longer than usual. Big Jim could hardly put one foot in front of the other. At last, the little procession reached the gallows and it then took only a second or two to place the noose around the man's neck and send him through the trapdoors. In his memoirs, Ellis remarked that Hargreaves's execution was, 'a bad day's work'.

Most murders with pokers were of this kind; squalid domestic crimes of little interest in themselves. The following year though, there was a murder involving a poker which was a little out of the ordinary. Not only was the crime committed against a victim who was quite unknown to the killer, the execution itself was notable for not going as smoothly as might have been wished.

Louis Voison: The Bloomsbury Mystery

Hanged at Pentonville, 2 March 1918
At about 8:00 am on the morning of Friday, 2 November 1917, Mr T. G. Henry was on his way to work. He had previously been a nurse in an asylum, but had recently begin working in the packing department of a company which delivered parcels. Henry lived in central London, in a square in Bloomsbury called Regent Square, at the heart of which was a large garden surrounded by railings. As he passed the garden, Henry noticed a large bundle, wrapped up in sacking, that had evidently been thrown over the railings. Suspecting that this might be stolen property stashed there temporarily by a burglar, Henry climbed over the railings and investigated. To his horror, he discovered that the bundle contained a decapitated and legless corpse. The hands were also

missing. Nearby, he found another, smaller parcel, also wrapped in a sheet and sacking. This proved to contain a pair of human legs.

The police were summoned and an autopsy was conducted on the remains that very day. The body was found to be that of a woman aged about 30, who would in life have stood about 4ft 11in in height. She had been dead for perhaps 24 hours. The dismemberment had been carried out with great skill and the surgeon who examined the corpse during the post mortem, gave it as his opinion that some degree of medical knowledge might account for the skill with which the joints had been separated; either that or experience in butchering animals.

This sensational murder was dubbed 'The Bloomsbury Mystery' by the popular press, but it was not destined to remain a mystery for long. A cursory look at the material in which the body had been wrapped, led swiftly to the identification of the victim. On one of the sheets was stitched in red cotton a laundry mark, '11H', and a photograph of this was published in the newspapers. Almost at once, a laundry contacted the police, having recognised their mark. They said that it belonged to a customer of theirs called Emilienne Gerard, who was the wife of a French soldier. They were able to provide the police with this woman's address, which was a set of rented rooms in Munster Square, St Pancras, barely a mile from where the body had been found.

This was not the only clue which was to prove crucial in solving this gruesome case. Placed between the sheets and sacking which enveloped the body, had been a piece of torn, brown wrapping paper, upon which was written, 'Blodie Belgiam [sic]'. At first, this misled the police into supposing that the death might have had something to do with the German invasion of Belgium. Its real significance emerged when a suspect had been identified.

A search of Emilienne Gerard's flat at 50 Munster Square provided a good deal of evidence. On the table lay an IOU for £50, signed by somebody called Louis Voisin. A photograph of Voisin hung over the mantelpiece and it transpired that the rent of the place was paid by the same man. The landlady, Mary Elizabeth Rouse, was able to shed light on one minor mystery of the case, which was why the dead woman's hands had been cut off. Obviously, the head would be of great importance in identifying a corpse, which was presumably why the killer had removed it, but why take the hands? The explanation was simple; the hands too could have helped confirm the identity of the dead woman. One of Emilienne Gerard's hands had, according to her landlady, a prominent scar upon it which, she had told the landlady, had been caused by boiling fat. It seemed likely that this distinguishing mark had prompted the murderer to take the hands at the same time as the head and conceal them somewhere.

Emilienne Gerard had not been seen since the night of Wednesday, 31 October, when there had been a Zeppelin raid on London. Her landlady had no idea where she had gone, but mentioned that Mrs Gerard was very close to Louis Voisin, the man whose photograph hung above the mantlepiece at 50, Munster Square. It was in fact common knowledge in the neighbourhood that Voisin was Mrs Gerard's lover and that he spent a good deal of time at her flat.

So far, the whole investigation had taken just 48 hours and when it was learned that Louis Voisin was a well-known butcher in that part of London, the police were confident that they were on the right trail. Voisin lived at 101 Charlotte Street, only half a mile from both Regent Square and Munster Square. When officers knocked on Voisin's door, they found him in the company of another French woman called Bertha Roche. There was at this stage no actual evidence to connect either Voisin or the woman in his flat with the murder, but Detective Inspector Frederick Wensley, who was in charge of the case, thought that he needed to interview both of them and so took them with him to Bow Street police station. The fact that neighbours said that they had heard the voice of more than one woman in the basement of Voisin's flat on the night of the air raid on 31 October led Wensley to suspect that both Voisin and Bertha Roche might know something about the disappearance of Emilienne Gerard.

At this stage, it was not even certain that the human remains found in Regent Square were actually those of the missing French woman and Louis Voisin laughed at the idea when he was being interviewed. He freely admitted knowing Mrs Gerard, but said that she had told him that she was going to go to France to see her husband. Voisin claimed that she had asked him to feed her cat while she was away. Inspector Wensley detained Voisin and his friend, whom he said was no more than a casual acquaintance, and continued his enquiries. Officers began going from door to door in the area around Munster Square and soon found a man who had had dinner with Emilienne Gerard on the night of 31 October. She had said nothing to him that night about going to France.

The next morning, Wensley resumed his questioning of Voisin, via an interpreter. He asked if the suspect would have any objection to writing the words, 'Bloody Belgium'. Louis Voisin agreed and when given a pencil and paper, wrote at once, 'Blodie Belgiam'. Of one thing Wensley was now certain: the man sitting opposite him was involved in some way with the dismembered corpse which had been dumped in Bloomsbury. He obtained a search warrant and sent one of his men, Detective Sergeant Collins to search 101 Charlotte Street.

A door led from the kitchen at Voison's home to a cellar. When he entered this dark room, almost the first thing which Sergeant Collins found was a tub of sawdust. Thrusting his hands incautiously into the sawdust, he found to his horror that it contained a human head. Not only was there the head of Emilienne Gerard buried in the sawdust, it also contained both her hands. Having made this gruesome discovery, Collins realised that it was time to call in experts to examine the premises. Bernard Spilsbury, perhaps the most famous pathologist of the twentieth century was, even in those early days of his career, a household name in Britain. His patient and methodical approach had ended in the hanging of Dr Crippen and also been instrumental in the conviction of the George Smith; the so-called 'Brides in the Bath' killer. Now, Spilsbury set out to reconstruct the death of the women whose mutilated body had been thrown over the railings of a London garden as though it was a bag of rubbish.

One matter which complicated things somewhat was that Voisin was in the habit of slaughtering sheep and calves in his kitchen, which meant that there were naturally many bloodstains about the place. Even a hundred years ago though, it was possible for a forensic scientist to distinguish between animal blood and that of humans. Spilsbury found that the kitchen was bespattered with human blood. It was on the floor, up the walls and even on the ceiling. From the amount of blood he found in the basement of 101 Charlotte Street, he deduced that Mrs Gerard had been killed and dismembered there. This was enough for Inspector Wensley, who charged both Louis Voisin and Bertha Roche with the murder of Emilienne Gerard.

Before the trial began at the Old Bailey in February 1918, the police had pieced together what they thought was a fairly accurate picture of the ghastly events of the night of 31 October 1917. Mrs Gerard, frightened by the air raid, had gone to see her lover. She was aware of the existence of Bertha Roche, who was the other mistress of Louis Voisin. Roche did not however know about Emilienne Gerard. When the senior of the two mistresses arrived at the basement flat in Charlotte Street, she found Voisin in bed with Bertha Roche. There was, not surprisingly, some sort of quarrel and the upshot was that Roche seized a poker and began beating the other woman around the head with it. The attack had been a frenzied one, the decapitated head of the victim showing many bruises and abrasions. At some point, Voisin had taken a hand and when one of his lovers was laying dead upon the floor, he decided to cut up her body as though she had been one of the sheep which he regularly butchered there.

The trial saw one of the most implausible explanations ever advanced by a defendant in a murder case to exculpate himself. According to Voisin's account of the night, he had gone to visit Mrs Gerard and found the door to her flat to be unlocked. Upon entering, he had noticed that his lover's head and hands were laying on the kitchen table. There was no sign of the rest of the body and so, for reasons which were never fully explained, he took the head and hands home with him and hid them in his cellar.

Mr Justice Darling, the judge in the trial of Louis Voisin and Bertha Roche, ruled that the woman could not properly be tried for murder and he remanded her to stand trial later on a charge of being an accessory after the fact. In other words, he felt that the evidence showed that Roche had taken no part in the murder, but had helped her lover to clear up afterwards. In fact, this was almost certainly the precise opposite of what had actually happened.

Having put forward such a ludicrous explanation for the body parts found in his cellar, it was perhaps inevitable that the jury should find Louis Voisin guilty of murder. Although an interpreter had been present during the trial, Mr Justice Darling had sufficient command of French to pronounce sentence of death in that language. The execution was at first fixed for 26 February 1918, but the Home Office ordered a brief delay, because they did not wish to see Voisin hanged before the trial of his mistress. It was thought possible that he might be needed as a witness.

Bertha Roche's trial for being an accessory after the fact of murder, took place at the Old Bailey on 1 March 1918. It was clear that the woman in the dock had been present during the murder and had, at the very least, been involved in cleaning up afterwards and helping Voison dispose of the body. After she had been convicted, Bertha Roche had a fit of hysterics, denying that she had even known Emilienne Gerard. The judge, Mr Justice Avory, waited until she had calmed down and then said simply, 'The sentence upon you is that you be kept in penal servitude for seven years.' It was a severe sentence, for reasons at which we shall later look. After the trial was over, Mr Justice Avory made a cryptic observation to the prosecution counsel. 'I presume,' he said, 'that there are other facts connected with the crime that have not been made public?' The barrister agreed that this was so.

On the very day that Bertha Roche was sent to prison for her part in the murder, John Ellis arrived at Pentonville prison to hang Louis Voisin. As soon as he got to the prison, he was able to see the man he would be executing the next day, as Voisin was being taken to be weighed. Two things struck the executioner about the man on the scales. The first was that Voisin was very short, only five feet three inches. The second was that the man appeared to have no neck at all to speak of. This was naturally of interest, because of the implications for the placing of the noose the next day. As far as Ellis could see, the condemned prisoner's chin hardly jutted out at all from the remarkably thick and bull-like neck.

Taking into account Voison's height and weight, Ellis decided upon a drop of six feet. He really wished to make it a little longer than this, but already he had exceeded the Home Office table by five inches and was worried that the doctor or under sheriff would object if he increased it any further. As it was, everybody concerned agreed that six feet would be an acceptable length for the drop the next morning.

At ten minutes to nine on the morning of 2 March 1918, the hushed group of officials waited outside Voisin's cell. From within, they could hear the condemned man raving like a lunatic; alternately sobbing, weeping and raging angrily. The doctor entered the cell and offered Voisin a large glass of brandy to steady his nerves. At first, the man who was about to die apparently only took a sip, because those standing outside the cell heard the doctor say firmly, 'Drink it all up!' When the prison clock began striking the hour, the hangman went in to prepare Voisin. There were two chaplains present and the man who had been involved in such a bloody murder was crying helplessly like a small child. In his hands was a handkerchief which was wringing wet with the tears which he had shed. Ellis assistant removed this from Voisin's hand and indicated that the man should stand up.

The presence of not one but two priests in the confines of the condemned cell complicated matters, because as his spiritual advisors moved, so too did Voisin move with them, making it tricky to fasten his hands behind his back. Eventually, this was done and the procession was ready to move to the scaffold.

Long experience of such things had led John Ellis to believe that here was a man who might very well faint before the lever was pulled and the trapdoors fell. This made him anxious to hurry things along. He walked briskly to the waiting noose and left it to his assistant to escort Voisin to the gallows. It was clear to everybody that the Frenchman was at the last extremity. He could not stand upright and began swaying all over the place. Ellis signalled to two warders to support Voisin while he attempted to fasten the noose. This was easier said than done, because just as he had feared, Voisin's stout neck made this very difficult. There was hardly any protruding chin or jawbone and the hangman was afraid that the noose might slip over the head when Voisin plummeted through the trapdoors. To ensure that this mishap did not occur, he pulled the noose far tighter than was his usual practice. So far gone was Louis Voisin though, that he hardly seemed to notice.

As soon as the rope was in place, Ellis indicated that everybody should leave the scaffold and he darted to the lever. It was a great relief to him when he saw that the hanging had gone as smoothly as usual and that Voisin had died instantly. The governor congratulated Ellis afterwards upon the efficiency with which he had carried out the execution. 'Very quick!', he observed.

Berthe Roche went mad in prison and died before completing her sentence. The autopsy on Emilienne Gerard showed that he had been subjected to a flurry of relatively light blows, which together probably resulted in her death. Voisin was a powerful man with strong musculature. It is unlikely that he would have needed to rain many blows down on a woman's scalp with a piece of metal, in order to kill her. Nor did he have any obvious motive for murder. In the years following the execution of Voisin, it was said that perhaps the wrong person had been hanged for murder. It seems quite possible that it was Berthe Roche who killed Mrs Gerard and Voisin who decided to cover up the crime by putting his skill as a butcher to good use. The problem was that the aftermath of the murder was so hideous that it might have prejudiced the court against the burly man in the dock; the man who had without doubt chopped off a woman's head and otherwise mutilated her body, even if she was dead at the time.

Arthur de Stamir (Stamrowsky): The Man Hanged for the Sake of an Old Raincoat

Hanged at Wandsworth, 12 February 1918

Captain Edward Tighe was connected with an old and prosperous Irish family. In 1917, he was living quietly in Wimbledon, a district in south London. Captain Tighe suffered greatly from asthma and would sometimes get up in the night and move about, in an attempt to relieve the distressing breathlessness which is the main symptom of this condition. Early in the morning of Tuesday, 13 November 1917, Eva Mary Parfit, a housemaid, heard groaning from Captain Tighe's room and on investigating, found the captain laying on the floor, covered in blood. At first, it was thought that he had fallen over in the night and injured himself, but when the doctor was summoned, he saw at once that this was no accident. Captain Tighe had been viciously assaulted, beaten round the head so forcefully with a poker that the steel rod had actually been bent out of shape.

After Tighe had been removed to the local hospital, the police began to investigate and ascertain what had happened. A window at the rear of the house seemed to have been forced and it was theorised that the captain had disturbed a thief on the premises and been attacked by the man as he tried to escape. Nothing was missing from the house, other than an old mackintosh and a cheap, tin pocket watch. It was supposed that the mackintosh had been taken to cover up the bloodstains which must have covered the murderer's clothes. Four days later, Edward Tighe died without regaining consciousness and the police launched a murder enquiry. The only difficulty that they faced was that there were absolutely no clues as to who might have committed the dreadful crime.

Almost a month passed, without any progress being made in the inquiry into Captain Tighe's death. The police were on the point of scaling down the investigation, when there was an amazing piece of luck. A pawnbroker in Streatham, a London district which is not far from Wimbledon, contacted the local police station and told them that a man had tried to sell him some silverware. He had asked the man to call back later. The police staked out the shop and arrested a man carrying £200-worth of silver plate, the proceeds of a recent robbery in Streatham.

The man arrested at the pawnbroker's shop gave his name as Arthur Harold Victor de Stamir, although his real name was Stamrowsky. He was a French citizen who had been brought to this country by his parents at the age of three. When his home was searched, Captain Tighe's mackintosh was found there, together with the almost valueless watch which had also been taken on the night of the murder.

Stamrowsky or de Stamir was now in an exceedingly tight spot. How did he explain the presence of these incriminating articles in his lodgings? Let us see what the defence was that he presented when he found himself on trial for murder before Mr Justice Darling on 10 January 1918.

According to Stamrowsky's version of events, he had on 7 November 1917, met an Australian soldier called Reginald Fisher. Fisher had suggested that the two of them carry out a burglary and Winkfield Lodge, Captain Tighe's house, the selected target. After forcing an entry, the two of them had gone upstairs and entered Tighe's bedroom. He had woken up and the Australian had picked up a poker and struck him over the head to silence him. Then he had taken the mackintosh to cover up his bloodstained uniform.

If this all sounded a little thin, the rest of the story was even less plausible. Two days later, Stamrowsky met up with Reginald Fisher and the two of them agreed that it was best if they did not see each other again. Before leaving, the Australian had sold Stamrowsky the Captain's mackintosh for ten shillings!

The jury took no time at all to deliver their verdict of guilty, adding a rider to the effect that they did not believe that Reginald Fisher had ever existed. Stamarowsky was then sentenced to death. There was no appeal and the execution was fixed for 12 February 1918.

The executioner usually arrived at the prison at 4:00 on the afternoon before the execution, but on this occasion Ellis got there an hour earlier, because the sheriff had asked to be present when the gallows were prepared. This was an unusual request, but Ellis saw no reason not to comply. The warders told him that Stamrowsky was a pretty cold blooded character, as shown by the following anecdote. He was a heavy smoker and when visiting Stamrowsky in his cell, the chaplain had remarked upon the heavy nicotine stains on the man's fingers. Stamrowsky had laughed and replied, 'So what? It will all be burned away by chloride of lime in a few days.' This was a reference to the fact that executed prisoners were buried in quicklime.

As usual, John Ellis intended to give the condemned man a rather longer drop than that recommended in the Home Office guidelines. (See Appendix 3 for a discussion of this subject.) The prison doctor was present while Ellis was measuring the rope for the execution the next day and asked what length of drop he proposed to give. When told that it would be seven feet, which was five inches over the figure in the official table, the doctor asked, 'Don't you think that's too much?' Purporting to misunderstand him, Ellis merely answered, 'Yes, quite sufficient.'

Right up to the last minute, Stamrowsky gave the impression of a man not especially bothered by what was about to befall him that day. At breakfast on the day of his execution, he asked if he could have something extra and was given two new laid eggs, which he ate with relish. Because it was wartime and things were sometimes a little chaotic, Ellis did not have an assistant at this hanging, which mean that the man to be executed would not have his feet fastened together when he was standing on the scaffold. When Ellis entered the cell, the Roman Catholic chaplain was sitting with Stamrowsky. The condemned man stood up at once, as soon as he saw the hangman entering the cell. Ellis fastened his wrists behind his back and whispered to him, 'Put your feet together at once when we get there and I'll have it over as quickly as possible.' Stamrowsky replied cheerfully, 'Righto!'

The procession, consisting of the sheriff, warders, chaplain, hangman and prisoner, walked to the scaffold, which was only a few yards away. As he had been requested to do, Stamrowsky placed his feet together when he was standing on the trapdoors and John Ellis pulled the white hood over the man's face and placed the noose about his neck. Then he turned and went to the lever which operated the trapdoors. He pulled the lever and sent Stamrowsky plummeting to his death.

As soon as the execution was over, the doctor arrived and then descended into the pit beneath the gallows to check that the hanged man was in fact dead. He climbed back out in a state of great excitement and declared to Ellis, in front of everybody, 'Ellis, this wasn't good enough! You didn't give him enough drop.' The executioner reminded him that if the doctor had had his way, then Stamrowsky would have had even less of a drop. It was a terrible situation, because instead of dying cleanly from a broken neck, the man hanging at the end of the rope was choking to death. There was nothing that could be done about it though.

A short time later, the doctor sought Ellis out and apologised. What had happened was a common enough event at executions. The principal warder had explained to the doctor that in the time that it took for the hangman to turn and go to the lever, Stamrowsky had fainted clean away. He had been dropping to the floor when the trapdoors opened and this meant that he did not get the full drop that had been planned. It was unfortunate, but no fault of the hangman.

Chapter Four

Prisoners in the Tower: The Shooting of Spies

It is intriguing to note that although we tend often to associate the Tower of London with sixteenth-century beheadings such as Anne Boleyn and Lady Jane Grey, more people were actually executed in the Tower during the first two years of the First World War than throughout the whole of the Tudor dynasty. Between 1485, when Henry VII, the first Tudor monarch, came to power and 1603, when Elizabeth I, the last of the Tudors, died, six men and women were executed at the Tower of London. Eleven spies were, on the other hand, shot in the Tower in the eighteen months between November 1914 and April 1916.

The use of firing squads to deal with soldiers facing the death penalty has been customary in this country since the English Civil War. It was only logical after the outbreak of war in 1914 to adopt this method of execution to deal with men convicted of offences relating to military matters. Most people are aware of the execution by firing squad of cowards and deserters on the Western Front in France, but not everybody realises that men were also being shot at dawn during this same time in the very heart of London.

There was for almost 200 years a convention that executions by military firing squad should take place only overseas. This custom was, by and large, adhered to during the First World War. For instance, deserters from the Western Front who succeeded in returning to this country were not court martialled and shot in England when they were recaptured. They were rather taken back to France to be executed there. The problem arose with the spies who were caught in Britain and sentenced to death, almost invariably by courts martial. Since they had been tried and sentenced by military courts, it was only fitting and proper that they should be shot, rather than hanged.

Nobody knows why the Tower of London was thought to be an appropriate place for the carrying out of executions. There were several army barracks in and around the capital which might easily have been used and would have resulted in less publicity; Wandsworth Military Detention Barracks, for instance. The choice of the Tower was probably influenced by the fact that it had in the eighteenth century been used on occasion for executions of this sort and had a permanent garrison of soldiers stationed within its walls. The story of the last executions to take place at the Tower of London before the First World War is told in Appendix 1.

Carl Lody: A Brave Man

Shot at the Tower of London, 6 November 1914

Spies are sometimes looked at a little askance in wartime; their activities being regarded as considerably less straightforward and honourable than those of ordinary soldiers in uniform on the front line. There seems to many people something a little shabby and underhand about disguising oneself as a civilian and creeping about behind enemy's lines. This feeling was very strong in the opening months of the First World War, when German spies were being seen behind every bush, and anybody bearing a name which sounded even the faintest bit Teutonic was at hazard of being reported to the authorities by the neighbours. In this feverish atmosphere, with German soldiers being blamed for bayoneting Belgian nuns, killing babies and all manner of other atrocities, it is all the more surprising that the first man actually convicted of spying for Germany was regarded with reluctant admiration in this country and was respected as a brave soldier, even by those whose job it was to execute him.

Carl Hans Lody was born in Berlin on 20 January 1877. In 1900, he joined the German navy, serving for a year, before being transferred to the naval reserve. He then worked on merchant ships, followed by a spell as a tour guide in Hamburg. Later, he moved to the United States and married an American woman. He also, in the process, became a fluent English speaker, albeit with a strong American accent. When war came, Lody volunteered to rejoin the navy, but Germany's naval intelligence department thought that a fluent English speaker with an American passport would be of more use to them in Britain. An American tourist called Charles Inglis was in Berlin in August 1914 and applied for a visa to enable him to travel round Europe. His passport ended up in the German Foreign Office, where it was 'lost'.

In fact it was passed to naval intelligence, where Lody's photograph was substituted for that of Charles Inglis. When Carl Lody stepped ashore in England on 27 August 1914, nobody would ever have guessed that he was really German.

The focus of Germany's intelligence services in this country during the First World War was naval activity and the preparedness of the British fleet. It was, in a war where blockading of ports was practiced and mastery of the high seas essential, of the utmost importance to know where the enemy's ships were anchored, when they sailed and what protection was being afforded to the ports.

Historically, Britain's navy has been based in the south of the country, in readiness to counter threats from Britain's traditional enemies, France and Spain. This meant that ships were to be found in Chatham and Portsmouth. With the growing military rivalry between Britain and Germany in the early years of the twentieth century, particularly in the field of strongly armoured battleships, it was thought necessary to move the main base of naval activity further north, for speedier access to the North Sea. When war began in 1914, the British Grand Fleet moved to an anchorage at Scapa Flow in the Orkney Islands. Scotland thus became the place to go if one wished to keep an eye on British naval activity.

On 14 August 1914, just ten days after Britain's declaration of war on Germany, Carl Lody travelled from Hamburg to Norway, which was a neutral country. From there, he took a ship to Newcastle, in the north of England, arriving in this country on 27 August. He then made his way at once to Edinburgh and booked into a hotel there.

Edinburgh was the perfect base for anybody wishing to spy on British shipping. Royal naval vessels were moored in the Firth of Forth, the estuary of the River Forth. The approach to the sea was mined and guarded with gun emplacements and ships carried out sorties from here into the North Sea. It was Lody's job to report on the defences around the Firth of Forth, as well as the disposition of naval forces in the estuary. Of particular interest to his bosses in German intelligence was details of any damage suffered to ships following engagements with German forces.

Unfortunately for Lody, he had not been very well briefed by his masters in Berlin, nor provided with the necessary materials to enable him to spy successfully. He had been given no codebooks, secret inks or anything else which would allow him to communicate securely with his superiors. Nor had he been warned of the precautions being taken by the British to protect themselves against enemy agents. For example, nobody had told him that letters and telegrams to and from Britain were all scrutinised by the censors. Since he was sending all his communications in plain text, written in English and German, it was inevitable that he should soon come to the attention of the Special Branch. It did not help matters that the main contact to whom he was sending information was a certain Adolf Burchard, in Stockholm. It was known that this man was an agent of German naval intelligence, whose real name was Leipziger. Those responsible for censoring letters leaving Britain noted at once when a telegram was sent to Burchard from Scotland. It was written in English and signed using the identity under which Lody was travelling; that of the American, Charles Inglis.

From Edinburgh, Lody journeyed to London and then returned to Scotland. He went from there to Liverpool and then took a ship for Ireland. The first two communications he sent to Stockholm were allowed through by the censors. Two further reports were stopped, because they contained sensitive information which would have proved useful to Germany. These letters were written in German and were about as compromising as could be. For instance, one communication which was intercepted and not allowed to proceed to the spymaster in Stockholm said:

In the North Sea, as far as I can ascertain, 22 small vessels have been sunk. Also that a small cruiser is lying at Leith. And 4 armed cruisers and about 10 torpedo boats and 2 destroyers are laying at Grangemouth

It is hard to imagine anybody other than a spy writing such a letter.

One letter which was passed gleefully by the censors and allowed to continue on its way to Adolf Burchard was a long account which Lody sent about the landing of Russian troops in Scotland. Readers might be aware that a ludicrous rumour swept Britain in 1914 that the Russians had landed. There were stories of how they had been seen stamping the snow from their boots and demanding vodka in Scottish pubs. Since there was not a word of truth in the increasingly mad tales being spun about this, Special Branch were happy for this particular piece of misinformation to find its way to Berlin. The letter he sent was as follows:

Will you kindly communicate with Berlin at once by wire (code or whatever system at your disposal) and inform them that on Sept. 3rd great masses of Russian soldiers have passed through Edinburgh on their way to London and France. Although it must be expected that Berlin has knowledge of these movements, which probably took its start at Archangel, it may be well to forward this information. It is estimated here that 60,000 men have passed, numbers which seem greatly exaggerated. I went to the depot [station] and noticed trains passing through at high speed, blinds down. The landing in Scotland took place at Aberdeen.

Yours very truly
Charles

Once he reached Dublin, Carl Lody booked into the Gresham Hotel, where a number of Americans were staying. From there, he wrote to his contact in Sweden, saying that he was beginning to feel nervous and worried that he was being followed. It was perfectly true that he was being followed; plainclothes officers had kept Lody under constant observation for almost the whole of the time that he was in the United Kingdom. On 2 October, the spy left Dublin, heading for Killarney and most likely heading towards the naval base at Queenstown, but the authorities felt that they had more than enough evidence against Carl Lody and the Royal Irish Constabulary were instructed to detain him.

Carl Lody was taken back to England and imprisoned in London's Wellington Barracks, under the watchful eyes of the 3rd Battalion of the Grenadier Guards. There then arose the question of how to deal with this, the first German spy to be arrested in Britain during the First World War. The first point to be decided was whether Lody should be tried by a military or civilian court. There was some vacillation about this, but the eventual decision was that a court martial would be the best way of handling the case. The second point was what law had been broken and what the charges should be. Considering that here was an enemy spy caught red-handed in wartime, it might surprise some readers to learn that it was not at all clear just what crime, if any, Carl Lody had committed.

The most obvious course would have been to charge Lody under either the Official Secrets Act or the recently passed Defence of the Realm Act, popularly known by the acronym DORA. The problem was that until it was amended on 27 November 1914, it was not possible to impose the death sentence. The maximum punishment possible under the Official Secrets Act was seven years on each count. The intention was that Lody should be executed, and so he actually faced two counts of war treason. This meant that he was technically being tried under international law, rather than for any putative breach of British, domestic law. The legality of this move was open to question, but it was felt necessary to make it explicitly plain that any person wanting to carry out espionage in this country might expect to face the death penalty. In the event, this was the only prosecution for war treason of the whole war. It was also the only spy trial to be conducted publicly.

The court martial of Carl Lody for two charges of war treason took place at the Middlesex Guildhall in Westminster over the course of three days, from 30 October to 2 November 1914. The Director of Public Prosecutions himself presented the case for the prosecution. Sir Achibald Bodkin showed that there was overwhelming evidence that Lody had been travelling around the British Isles making notes about naval and military matters and sending the information he had collected to a German agent in Sweden. The accused man made no attempt to deny any of this; but refused to confirm it either, lest he compromise his superiors or other agents in the field. This principled stand of a man who was prepared to sacrifice his own life rather than cooperate with his captors won him reluctant admirations from everybody in the court.

After sentence of death by shooting was passed, the condemned man was transferred from Wellington Barracks to the Tower of London. There had not been an execution at the Tower of London since the middle of the eighteenth century and it is not known why it was thought to be a suitable place to execute a man by firing squad. When he arrived at the Tower, having been told of the sentence, Carl Lody knew that he had only twelve hours to live. Many men in such a position all but go to pieces, but not Carl Lody. He was keen to put his affairs in order and write one or two final letters. These must surely rank as being among the most self-possessed communications ever penned by a man who knew that this was the last evening of his life. The first of these letters was addressed to the commanding officer of the 3rd Battalion of the Grenadier Guards, expressing his appreciation for the treatment which he had received while held at their barracks. It read:

Sir,

I feel it my duty as a German officer to express my sincere thanks and appreciation towards the staff of officers and men who were in charge of my person during my confinement. Their kind and considered treatment has called my highest esteem and admiration as regards good fellowship even towards the enemy and if I may be permitted, I would thank you for making this known to them.

The other letter which Lody wrote on that grim November evening was to his mother and sister:

My dear ones,

I have trusted in God and He has decided. My hour has come, and I must start on the journey through the Dark Valley like so many of my comrades in this terrible War of Nations. May my life be offered as a humble offering on the altar of the Fatherland.

A hero's death on the battlefield is certainly finer, but such is not to be my lot, and I die here in the Enemy's country silent and unknown, but the consciousness that I die in the service of the Fatherland makes death easy.

The Supreme Court-Martial of London has sentenced me to death for Military Conspiracy. Tomorrow I shall be shot here in the Tower. I have had just Judges, and I shall die as an Officer, not as a spy.

Farewell. God bless you.

One thing which the Tower of London did have which made it a suitable site to carry out an execution by firing squad was an indoor rifle range. It was in this nondescript structure, which was in the outer ward, between the Constable and Martin Towers, that Carl Lody would meet his death at dawn on 6 November. There would be eight members of the firing party; soldiers who had been chosen at random.

At first light on 6 November, the Assistant Provost-Marshal, Lord Athlumney, came to Lody's cell with a military escort, to lead him to his death. Lody said diffidently to this official, 'I suppose that you will not care to shake hands with a German spy?' At once, Lord Athlumney put out his hand, saying, 'No, but I will shake hands with a brave man.'

It was afterwards remarked by witnesses that of all those present, Lody himself appeared to be the one who was most at ease. According to one of the Beefeaters who saw the procession as it made its way to the firing range, Lody strolled along with as little concern as if he had been on his way to a tea party. The chaplain, who walked at the condemned man's side, seemed very affected by the situation and his voice was breaking with emotion. When they reached the door to the rifle range, the chaplain was so upset that he turned in the wrong direction. With a smile, Lody took the priest's arm and guided him through the door of the gloomy little building. It was the most natural action imaginable, but showed that the one man whom one might reasonably expect to be the most upset and disturbed that morning, was actually the calmest and most collected of all.

Once inside the 25-yard-long range, things moved swiftly. Lody was fastened to an ordinary wooden kitchen chair. He refused to have his eyes bound, saying that he wished to die with his eyes open. At the word of command, the firing party cocked their weapons, took aim and fired at the seated man's heart, as though it had been no more than one of the paper targets at which they were used to exercising their marksmanship. It was reported in the press that the executed man had been buried within the precincts of the Tower, but this was untrue. In fact, he was interred in the East London Cemetery at Plaistow.

Carl Lody's trial and execution are notable for a number of reasons. In the first place, this was the only such trial held during either of the world wars which was conducted in public. All the rest were held *in camera*. It was also the only trial for war treason to take place in Britain. Lody's case was singular for another reason. He was a German national who had voluntarily come to an enemy country because he conceived it to be his patriotic duty to do so. The other men who were arrested for espionage were either not

German nationals or had less admirable reasons for spying than simple patriotism towards their country. A number seem to have been motivated more by cupidity than patriotism.

Carl Muller: 'I am writing this from 201.'

Shot in the Tower of London, 23 June 1915

Not all those who were charged and convicted of espionage during the First World War were executed. Some were sent to prison, while others received a death sentence which was later commuted to a term of imprisonment. Although no woman was executed in Britain during the course of the war, Eva de Bournonville, a Swedish national, was actually sentenced to death for spying. She was, however, reprieved and the sentence commuted to life imprisonment. Her story is told at the end of this chapter.

Another instance of an accused spy who ended up in prison, rather than facing a firing squad, occurred in early 1915, three months after Carl Lody's execution. The man concerned, a baker of German origin called Peter Hahn, was exceedingly lucky. Because he was a British subject, Hahn demanded, and was accorded, a civil trial at the Old Bailey. It was perhaps this which saved his life, although his companion and fellow conspirator was less fortunate.

Following Carl Lody's capture and execution, which resulted from his writing to a known German agent in Scandinavia, the German intelligence services changed tactics and began using commercial premises in neutral Holland as *poste restante* addresses where those working under cover in Britain could send their reports. In early 1915, the censors in Britain, who opened and examined with particular thoroughness all correspondence being sent to these known centres for espionage, read a seemingly innocuous letter which had been posted in the south London district of Deptford. It was addressed to an office in Amsterdam known to be used by Germany's naval intelligence, and on being heated in front of a fire, proved to have an additional message written in invisible ink. This said, 'C has gone to Newcastle and so am writing this from 201 instead.' Letters had already been intercepted to the address in Amsterdam, giving details of shipping moored in various British ports. It seemed likely that although the handwriting in this letter was different from the others, there might well be a connection between this and the others.

Special Branch detectives gave considerable thought as to what '201' might signify. It was possible that this was a house number and so a telephone call was made to Deptford police station. The officers at Scotland Yard asked how many streets in Deptford went up as high as 201. The reply was that only one street in that part of London had such a high number and that was Deptford High Street. When it was discovered that 201 Deptford High Street was the premises of a baker whose parents were German, Special Branch were sure that their hunch had been correct. A warrant was obtained to search the address. In the back room of the baker's shop was found a kit for writing messages in invisible ink. The baker, whose name was Hahn, was arrested.

When questioned, Peter Hahn refused to tell the police who 'C' might be. In fact after answering a few questions to establish his identity, Hahn clammed up and would not tell the officers any more. Enquiries among the baker's neighbours were more rewarding. They found that although Hahn had been born in Britain, he had spent much of his early youth living in Germany with his parents' families. They also discovered that a tall, Russian-looking man had been seen visiting Peter Hahn and that this man had spent nights at 201 Deptford High Street. The name of this individual was Muller. A piece of paper was found at Hahn's home which proved to have an address written on it in invisible ink. This was 38 Guildford Street in Bloomsbury, not far from the British Museum. When the police visited 38 Guildford Street, they found it to be a boarding house and one of the residents was a Mr C. Muller.

Everything was now falling neatly into place for the men from Special Branch. So far, their investigations had been almost a textbook case of patient police work. They could hardly believe their luck when the landlady at Guildford Street told them that Mr Muller had gone up to Newcastle for a few days. Luckily, she had a forwarding address for him.

Carl Muller had been born in 1857 in the town of Libau, at that time in the Russian Empire. He was an accomplished linguist, speaking Russian, German, English and Dutch. He had hardly a trace of an accent in any of these languages. After a varied career, Muller settled down in the Belgian town of Antwerp. By 1914, he was in financial difficulties over his business dealings and it was while finding a way to alleviate these that he agreed to undertake an espionage mission for Germany. His motive appears to have been wholly mercenary.

On 9 January 1915, Carl Muller boarded a ship in Rotterdam which took him to Hull. From there, he took a train south to London and booked into the boarding house at 38 Guildford Street. He already knew Peter Hahn, having met him when Hahn was living in Germany. The bakery was not doing very well and so Hahn was ready to allow his shop to be used as a base for Muller's activities, in exchange for a considerable sum in cash. Muller stored the tools of his trade at the shop in Deptford and received letters there. In January and February, he travelled around the coast, gathering information about the disposition of British warships along the east coast.

Because he was a British subject and not a foreign soldier, Peter Hahn was entitled to be tried not by court martial, as were most of the spies caught during the war, but by a civilian court. Due to the fact that the cases against the two men were inextricably linked, it was thought convenient to deal with them both at a single trial, which is why Carl Muller, unusually for a foreign spy, was tried at the Old Bailey.

On 2 June 1915, Peter Hahn and Carl Muller appeared together before the Lord Chief Justice. Both men faced charges under the amended Defence of the Realm Act, charges which could carry the death penalty. Hahn though had cooperated with the police after realising how serious was the situation in which he found himself. He had given all the information he could regarding Carl Muller and his activities and in addition to this, he had agreed to plead guilty. As a consequence, he escaped the firing squad and was instead sent to prison for seven years. Muller was clearly the instigator of the spying and had merely used his previous acquaintance with Hahn to lure the baker into his schemes. Muller was sentenced to death by firing squad.

Having seen the favourable impression that Carl Lody had made on the British public by his courageous behaviour, the government was determined that nothing of the sort should be allowed to happen with other German spies who might be captured. For this reason, Carl Muller's trial had been held *in camera* and no members of the public had been permitted in the court. The intention was that a brief statement would be issued after the execution and that would be the end of the matter. Things did not work out as planned though.

On 21 June, Muller's appeal against his conviction was dismissed. Since February, he had been held in Brixton prison, but now he was to be taken to the Tower of London for his appointment with the firing squad. At noon on Tuesday, 22 June, two military policemen came to the prison in a taxi to collect Muller. They intended to escort him to the Tower, where he would be lodged for the night, the plan being to execute him at dawn the next day. The taxi cab drove through south London and approached Tower Bridge. It then broke down. The sight of two soldiers guarding a foreign-looking prisoner was enough to attract a crowd, some of whom then began to shout that here was a German spy. In such a way, the news that another spy had been caught and was being taken to the Tower of London for execution soon spread throughout the capital, eventually even finding its way even into the American newspapers.

Carl Muller spent a very distressed night. He was not a young man, being only a few years short of 60, and was terrified of dying. He wept and wailed, repeatedly stating that he would dearly love to see his wife and children one last time. However, he rallied a little before dawn and when the time came for him to die, he had regained his composure. He managed to shake hands with the members of the firing squad and was able to meet death with some dignity. An army officer who was present at the execution subsequently wrote this account of the morning:

> On Wednesday 23 June at 6am, in the Miniature Rifle Range at the Tower, the prisoner was calm, shook hands with me and thanked me. I led him to the chair which was tied to short stakes driven into the ground, he sat on it quietly and the Sergeant buckled a leather strap round his body and the back of the chair and then blindfolded him with a cloth. The firing party consisted of eight guardsmen. I watched as closely as possible and went to him immediately after he was shot. I saw no expression of pain. I found no pulse and no sign of life. Death appeared to be instantaneous, and the body retained the same position. The bullets probably in fragments had passed through the thorax and out of the back. Some blood, mixed with what appeared to be bone, had escaped through the clothing and seven or eight drops had fallen to the ground.

Haicke Janssen and Willem Roos: 'Cigar Merchants'.

Shot at the Tower of London, 30 July 1915

The German intelligence services had not had much success in the opening months of the war and so decided upon a change in strategy. First, they began recruiting nationals of other countries, ranging from Sweden to Brazil; and secondly, they thought it worth disguising their agents as commercial travellers. In themselves, both ideas were perfectly sound; it was the fine details of the scheme which were unsatisfactory and led to the arrest of still more men operating as enemy agents.

On 12 May 1915, the SS *Estrom* docked in Hull, having travelled from neutral Holland. On board was a Dutch citizen by the name of Haicke Janssen. After spending a week in London, Janssen made his way to the port of Southampton. His cover was that of representative of a firm of cigar importers in the Hague, and, in theory, Janssen was looking for large orders of cigars, which he would pass to his head office, Dierks & Co. He was carrying with him boxes of cigars, which were supposedly samples of the wares which he was peddling. There would be no need to fool around with invisible inks or anything of that kind. All letters and telegrams would be sent in plain English, containing innocuous messages at which nobody would glance. What could be more natural for a commercial traveller taking orders for cigars than to send a telegram to his head office asking them to send 10,000 Cabanas or 3,000 Coronas?

Of course, the reference to cigars was simply a code. If sent from Portsmouth, then the 10,000 Cabanas meant that there were ten destroyers moored in the port. 'Coronas' was the code for battleships, 'Rothschilds' meant cruisers and so on. There was just one small flaw in this brilliant system of passing messages abroad about British naval deployments. British sailors certainly tended to be heavy smokers, but they invariably favoured pipes and cigarettes, rather than cigars. The idea of selling 10,000 Cabana cigars in Chatham or Portsmouth was utterly ludicrous. A telegram containing orders for such grotesquely large quantities of cigars, which were supposedly to be sold in and around the naval bases of Britain was in itself enough to attract the attention of the censors who read these communication being sent to the Netherlands.

The British secret service, like the Germans, maintained a network of agents who operated in the neutral countries of Holland and Scandinavia. The address to which the telegrams were being sent was checked and found to be a dingy little office, tucked away in a side street. It was clearly a front, an address where correspondence was sent to be forwarded elsewhere. Not only that, but Mr Dierkes was actually a German and strongly suspected to be working for German naval intelligence. As far as anybody was able to discover, no cigars were actually being dealt with by the office at Loosduinschekad in the Hague.

The British postal censors were intercepting and reading all the letters and telegrams being sent to Dierkes & Co. On 26 May 1915, Janssen sent a letter to his controller in the Hague, asking for 4000 Sumatra cigars. Two more letters followed, each detailing grotesquely large quantities of exotic cigars which were supposedly being ordered for shops in Southampton. On 30 May 1915, Haicke Janssen, who made no secret of his business as a commercial traveller and had registered with the authorities as soon as he had disembarked at Hull, was arrested in Southampton by Inspector Thomas McCormack. In his hotel room were various samples of cigars and a letter from his supposed employer. There was also an order book, which was completely empty, together with a Dutch passport. Later that same day, Detective Sergeant Bertram Sumpton from Scotland Yard escorted Janssen to London.

Haicke Janssen was not the only salesman operating in Britain on behalf of Dierks & Co. In the middle of May 1915, another Dutchman called Willem Roos arrived in London. He stayed only a couple of days in the capital, before taking a train north to Newcastle. From there, he travelled to Edinburgh. Like his fellow employee at the cigar importers, Roos limited his travelling to ports and naval bases. Like Janssen, Willem Roos was quite open about touring around the country and sending telegrams to his employer in Holland. He was shadowed by Special Branch detectives and on 2 June was arrested by Detective Inspector Albert Fitch. Among the papers he was carrying were pencil notes; map references of military installations which might have been of interest to Germany.

The two Dutchmen were taken to Scotland Yard, where they were questioned on 3 June. Janssen was the first to be interviewed. He seemed to know very little about cigars and admitted that his usual occupation was that of a sailor. He was quite unable to explain why anybody would have engaged him to sell cigars. He was asked whether or not he knew a man called Roos, to which he answered 'No'. After being questioned, Janssen was taken to another room.

Willem Roos was now invited to explain himself. Like Janssen, he was a sailor and did not appear to have a very extensive knowledge of cigars. He told the detectives that he and another man called Janssen were both employed by Dierks & Co. Asked if he would recognise Janssen, he at once agreed that he would. When Haicke Janssen was brought back into the room, he made gestures with his eyes and shook his head slightly; presumably indicating to the other man that they should not acknowledge each other. It was too late though and after a few more questions, the decision was made to charge both men under the Defence of the Realm Act. While they were being taken to Cannon Row police station, Roos dashed over to a door contained a glass panel. He smashed this and then sliced his arms across the jagged broken glass, hoping presumably to cut open his arteries and so end his life. Police officers administered first aid and he was taken for treatment at Westminster Hospital.

There was some confusion about where the arrested men should be held before their trial. At first, they were detained at the Tower of London, being kept in the part of the Tower known as the Casemates. It was thought to be very important that the two men should be allowed no chance to communicate before their trial. The Tower was not really ideal for use as a prison though and after four days they were transferred to the Military Detention Barracks at Wandsworth.

While he was in custody before facing court martial, Roos wrote to his sister, Clasina Roos, who was living in Holland. His bitterness towards Janssen is plain, for in the letter he said, 'Janssen can save my life if he tells the truth'. From the beginning, Willem Roos had believed that the only hope in saving his life was to cooperate fully with the police, which was why he freely admitted knowing Janssen. He blamed the other man for misleading the police about their knowing each other and thought that if this had led to his being charged with espionage.

The court martial of Haicke Janssen for espionage took place at the Middlesex Guildhall in Westminster on 16 July 1915. Evidence was given by experts that not only were the boxes in which Janssen was transporting his samples not suited to the task, but that some of the names of cigar types used in his telegrams were unknown. Janssen refused to make any statement or offer a defence to the charges against him and he was sentenced to death by shooting. The following day, Willem Roos was tried by the same court. While on remand in Brixton Prison, Roos had feigned madness, but examination by doctors suggested that he was not genuinely insane. At the end of the trial, he too was sentenced to death.

The execution of Janssen and Roos was notable for two reasons. In the first place, it was the only double shooting of the war, both men being executed within ten minutes of each other. It was also the only execution by firing squad which was not carried out in the indoor rifle range against the wall of the Tower. Instead, it took place in the dried-up moat which surrounds the Tower of London.

The two convicted spies were brought to the Tower by taxi cab on the morning of 29 July 1915. The government were anxious to avoid another such public scene as that which occurred when the taxi carrying Carl Muller broke down on the way to the Tower. The instructions sent to the officer in charge of the Wandsworth Military Detention Barracks by an official at the War Office said that:

The prisoners will be removed under suitable escort from Wandsworth Detention Barracks to the Tower of London early in the morning of 29th July. This removal should be effected in such a manner as to avoid publicity. The sentence should be carried out early in the morning of 30th July and as soon as it has been carried out a notification should be sent to this department when arrangements will be made for a communique to be sent to the press. No other communication on the subject is to be made to the public or the press.

Since the trials themselves had been held *in camera*, this meant that nobody would learn anything about the trial, nor the circumstances in which the men had been apprehended. All anybody would know was that two men had been shot for offences under the Defence of the Realm Act.

Their executions, at 6:00 am and 6:10 am the following day, went smoothly, due in part to the special arrangements which had been made. Four wooden stakes had been driven into the grassy floor of the moat and a wooden chair lashed to these, so that it would not topple over. The first to be shot was Janssen. Ten minutes later it was Willem Roos's turn. He asked that he might be granted the favour of finishing his cigarette and this was allowed. Then he too was secured to the chair with leather straps and died under the hail of bullets from the rifles of the firing party.

Ernst Melin: 'Possessing a Bottle Containing Lemon Juice'

Shot at the Tower of London, 10 September 1915
During the course of a fortnight, between the end of May and the beginning of June 1915, the Special Branch arrested seven people spying for Germany. Perhaps because of the suspicion aroused by anybody who appeared to be German at that time, the German intelligence services took to recruiting men and women from other countries, nations which were neutral. A typical example was Ernst Melin from Sweden.

Melin came from a very respectable background, his father having been a member of the Swedish parliament for many years and owner of a shipping company. For some reason, his son Ernst led a somewhat restless life and when he lost his job at a shipping line in 1915, the 49-year-old man drifted to Hamburg, where he was recruited as a spy. In January 1915, Ernst Melin arrived in England and took lodgings at Hampstead in London. He spent two weeks looking around and compiling a report of the military dispositions which he was able to see in the capital. Then he crossed the channel to the Netherlands and met with German agents there. They were impressed with what he had been able to discover in such a short time and it was agreed that Melin would return to Britain, where he would be paid £50 a month for his spying activities. This was a handsome enough wage, a century ago, but not perhaps worth risking one's life for.

On 26 February, Melin returned to England and began a tour of ports where the Royal Navy was operating. His cover was, however, to use the jargon of the espionage trade, 'blown'. While in Holland, he had met up with Mr Dierks, the supposed cigar importer who had employed Janssen and Roos. Although they lost sight of him from time to time, it was easy enough to prevent Melin's communications from reaching their intended recipients. The postal censors were scrutinising all telegrams and letters to the Netherlands and since Melin's were all addressed to a known German agent, it was not difficult to open these and check them for codes or secret writing.

Because of Melin's nationality and the fact that his father was Olaf Melin, an important man in Sweden, the Special Branch took their time in building up the case against him. If he was to be charged and ultimately executed, the British wished to be quite sure that they had plenty of evidence to justify such treatment of a citizen of a neutral country. It is this which accounts for the fact that Melin was left at large for so long. He had retained the same lodgings in Hampstead since first coming to Britain in January and although he vanished from time to time, it would have been easy enough to seize him at his home when he returned from his travels. In the event, it was not until 14 June 1915 that Detective Inspector Thomas Duggan knocked on the door of the house where Melin was staying in Hampstead and arrested him for offences under the Defence of the Realm Act.

In a sense, the authorities had been forced to act against Melin, because they could not leave at large any longer a man they were quite sure was spying on their country for the Germans. The evidence was not overwhelming and it was feared that there was a real chance that Melin might be acquitted. There was the extra complication that the Swedish embassy in London was taking a keen interest in the case and would be liable to object if one of their citizens were to be executed on what seemed to them to be flimsy or insufficient grounds.

To give some idea of the problems faced by the prosecution, when Ernst Melin's lodgings had been searched, the police had found a bottle of lemon juice. When asked what this was for, Melin replied that he used it for his complexion. This featured in one of the charges against him, namely:

Possessing a bottle containing lemon juice intended to be used for the purpose of communicating without lawful authority by means of invisible writing information intended to be communicated to the enemy.

This really was pretty thin. Clearly, one could lawfully possess a bottle of lemon juice for reasons other than espionage. The other charges were not very much more impressive: 'Having travelled from Rotterdam to Newcastle to collect information'; and 'sending newspapers having thereon certain written information from England'.

What had precipitated the decision to arrest Ernst Melin was that two parcels addressed to him had been intercepted; one posted in Tilbury and the other in Gravesend. These contained letters which appeared to be quite innocuous, until they were heated with an iron. Messages had been written in lemon juice, between the lines of the visible text. One such secret communication named several ships of the Royal Navy and urged Melin to gather information about them. It was impossible to leave a man sending and receiving letters of this sort to roam the country at will.

The Swedish embassy asked that a particular firm of lawyers be given access to Melin, who was being held at Wandsworth barracks. In the meantime, the prosecution was working hard to make sure that the case presented when Melin faced his court martial was as watertight as possible.

On 20 August, Ernst Melin's trial began at the Middlesex Guildhall. It was to last for two days and his defence team did all that they could. Although possession of a bottle of lemon juice was not in itself suspicious, the fact that the accused man also had in his home pen-nibs which had traces of lemon juice on them was enough to convince the court that he had been writing secret messages. That letters sent to him also had invisible writing on them, made with lemon juice, which was really too much of a coincidence. The man in the dock could offer no convincing explanation for his presence in Britain, nor how he was making his living. Melin was sentenced to death. The execution was to take place at the Tower of London on 10 September 1915.

It was remarked that Ernst Melin accepted his fate with resignation and was no trouble at all to those charged with guarding him. On the morning of 9 September, he was transferred to the Tower and shot the next morning at 6:00 am. By all accounts, he went to his death courageously, shaking hands with the men who would be shooting him and thanking his guards for their courtesy.

Augusto Roggen: The Man Who Should Have Stayed Out of the Witness Box

Shot at the Tower of London, 17 September 1915

Perhaps because they thought that non-Europeans might seem less suspicious to the British authorities, the German intelligence agencies recruited a number of agents from South America. The first of these men to be captured and executed was Augusto Roggen who, although born in Uruguay, was the son of a German and whose wife was also German. On 30 May 1915, Roggen came to Britain; ostensibly to examine, and possibly purchase, agricultural equipment.

After first visiting London, Augusto Roggen travelled north by train. His behaviour was very suspicious and he asked so many questions of the other passengers in the carriage, that they advised him not to go near the coast, for fear that he would be taken to be a spy. A little while later, when Roggen still insisted on asking questions about naval matters, those in his compartment became so hostile that he left the train at Lincoln, where he spent three days before continuing his journey to Scotland. He travelled to Edinburgh, partly, he said, for pleasure, but also to investigate the use of automobiles in farming. In other words, Roggen wanted to see how tractors compared to horses in agriculture. While in Edinburgh, Augusto Roggen posted two letters to an address in Holland. These were sent to a man called Heinrich Flores, who lived at Binnenweg 127, Rotterdam. These immediately caused the postal censors to alert Special Branch, because Flores was known to be an officer in the German navy.

By now, the British were fairly confident that they had identified yet another spy operating on behalf of Germany. They were content to let Roggen continue with his mission, wondering perhaps whether he might lead them to bigger fish. However, in early June 1915, the man they were watching left Edinburgh and moved north. He booked into the Tarbet hotel at Loch Lomond. Once he was settled in there, Roggen bought a map of Loch Lomond and the nearby Loch Long, which forms part of the Firth of Clyde. At this point, Special Branch knew that they had to act at once. Loch Long was the site of the Admiralty Torpedo Range and it was unthinkable that a known spy should be allowed to get within sight of the place. On 9

June 1915, Superintendent John Wright arrested Roggen and took him back to London for questioning.

As with Melin, the actual evidence against Augusto Roggen was not compelling. He had some liquids which might have been used for invisible writing, maps of Britain and a list of addresses in Holland. He was also found to be carrying a Browning automatic pistol. There was nothing to indicate though that he himself had actually carried out any acts of espionage.

The arrest and prosecution of Roggen was something of an embarrassment for the British government. The Uruguayan minister in London wished to be kept informed of the case against one of his citizens and so the court martial, which took place in August 1915, was conducted in the knowledge that the government of a neutral country was taking a close interest in the case. The four charges, all under the Defence of the Realm Act, were concerned not so much with espionage as such, but rather with the, 'doing of acts preparatory to the commission of an act prohibited under these regulations'. In other words, Roggen had been getting ready to spy on Britain and there was no evidence at all that he had actually broken any of the regulations set out in DORA.

Roggen's lawyers mishandled their client's case disastrously. The case for the defence was powerful. Augusto Roggen had correctly registered his address at all times in Britain and made no secret at all of his plans. There was nothing to suggest that he had collected any information and the 'fluid' which was supposedly to be used for invisible writing turned out to be nothing of the kind. Had the defence presented these facts and invited the court to acquit their client, it is entirely possible that Roggen would have walked free. However, his barristers did not advise the accused man that he had the right not to enter the witness box in order to be cross examined.

There were a number of things about Roggen and his activities which invited explanation. When he entered the witness box and began to be questioned by the prosecution, it was plain that he had no real explanation to offer for some of his actions. This created a bad impression on the court and led to his conviction. After all, why would a man on trial for his life not be eager and willing to clear up any matters which looked dubious? The answer is of course that anyone would be happy to offer such explanations, if they happened to be innocent.

The stumbling and evasive account which Roggen gave of some of his activities told heavily against him. He was sentenced to death and the date of the execution was fixed for 10 September, the same day that Ernst Melin was due to die. It looked as though another double execution, like that of Janssen and Roos, might be on the cards.

There was less than three weeks between the sentence of death being passed and the date set for Augusto Roggen to be shot. He appealed on several grounds, the chief of which was that his lawyers had not told him that he need not be cross examined in the witness box unless he chose. It is true that a refusal to enter the witness box sometimes tells against a defendant, but at the very least the option should be put to the person in the dock.

Roggen and his legal team were not the only ones trying to stave off his execution. The Uruguayan minister approached the Home Secretary and asked for a delay in the execution so that he could arrange for a petition to be sent, seeking clemency for Roggen. Minister Vidiella wished for another sentence to be substituted for the 'irreparable' one of death. This was something of a nuisance for the British government, who wrote back on 10 September, the day on which it was originally planned to shoot Augusto Roggen, announcing that the execution had been postponed. Arthur Nicolson, Under Secretary for Foreign Affairs, told the Uruguayan embassy that his fellow countryman had had a fair trial and that there was no chance of modifying the sentence unless the minister was able to present new information.

The affair was passed to the Ministry of War and they responded five days later by writing to Minister Vidiella, saying that the whole case had been scrupulously re-examined but that

the Secretary of State was unable under all the circumstances of the case to recommend to His Majesty any modification of the sentence passed by the court martial which heard the case.

On 17 September 1915, Augusto Roggen was led at 6:00 am to the miniature rifle range at the Tower of London. After shaking hands with the men who would be his executioners, he seated himself in the chair at one end of the range. He refused to be blindfolded and died instantly when seven bullets smashed into his chest. The coroner, who conducted a brief inquest on the day of the execution, recorded that Roggen had died of gunshot wounds and that his death was a case of 'justifiable homicide'. After a brief report of the execution appeared in the next day's *Daily Mail*, Roggen's wife wrote to the British authorities from Holland, asking if it would be possible to arrange for his corpse to be shipped across the channel, so that he might be buried in the Netherlands. Her request was granted.

There was a brief and melancholy coda to Augusto Roggen's death. Shortly after his execution, a steamer from Holland called at Newcastle, en route to Uruguay. The port officials, while examining the passenger lists, noticed the name of Roggen and were naturally intrigued. Dr Emilio Roggen was removed from the ship and brought ashore to be questioned by the police. He turned out to be Augusto Roggen's brother who was shocked and distressed to learn of his brother's ignominious death. It seemed that Dr Roggen, who had also been born in Uruguay and had dual Uruguayan and German nationality, had been staying in Germany when the war began. He had been conscripted and compelled to act as a medical officer in the field. It had taken him over eighteen months to escape and he was now on his way home to Uruguay. Satisfied that the man posed no threat to British interests, he was allowed to continue on his journey.

Fernando Buschman: The Penniless Spy

Shot at the Tower of London, 19 October 1915
The next spy to be executed at the Tower of London was another man with mixed Uruguayan and German antecedents. Fernando Buschman was a businessman with fingers in many pies. By his own account, he was the representative of a company in Brazil which dealt in a most eclectic variety of goods; ranging from bananas and potatoes to safety razors and guns.

On 14 April 1915, Buschman arrived in London and booked into the Piccadilly Hotel. He was evidently short of money, because after several nights, he moved to a cheaper hotel. At the same time, he began writing to the familiar address in the Hague, asking for money. The man to whom he wrote was the same Dierks who had supposedly been employing Willem Roos and Haicke Janssen to act as cigar salesmen. One of the strangest aspects of the German espionage against Britain during the opening years of the First World War is the sheer ineptitude of the methods used. The same addresses were used by almost all the spies and the same tiny group of men in Scandinavia or the Netherlands were invariably those with whom the secret agents were communicating. No effort was made by the Germans to alter their plans, or disguise the identities of the spymasters who were running the agents operating in Britain. This is odd, because the Germans were themselves censoring telegrams and letters leaving their own country; surely they must have realised that the British would be doing exactly the same?

Buschman's appeals for money became increasingly desperate, as he faced the very real prospect of being evicted from the hotel at which he was staying. In between begging for more money, he found time to travel to the south coast and visit Portsmouth and Southampton, presumably with a view to observing the Royal Navy ships in the two ports. Even his railway fares were proving a strain on Fernando Buschman's increasingly slender resources and when he returned to London, he made the fatal mistake of sending a telegram appealing for money, directly to 24 Plats, The Hague. This was an almost inconceivably stupid move, for although the telegram was apparently intended for a 'Madame de Klimm', the address to which it was sent was in fact the private residence of the German military attache in Holland, Colonel Osterdat. When this letter was intercepted by the authorities, the decision was made to arrest Buschman without further delay. At a little before midnight on 3 June 1915, Inspector George Riley of Scotland Yard knocked on the door of Buschman's hotel room and took him into custody. On the same day, a business associate of Buschman's called Emil Samuel Franco was also arrested and later charged with an offence under the Defence of the Realm Act.

The arrested businessman was passing himself off as a Brazilian, which provided one of the most solid pieces of evidence presented against him at his subsequent court martial. Close examination of his passport revealed that it was written in a hand very familiar to Special Branch. The handwriting belonged to none other than Heinrich Flores, the German intelligence agent who was based in Holland. A few enquiries at the Brazilian embassy confirmed what the investigating officers suspected, that the Brazilian passport under which Fernando Buschman was travelling was a forgery. There was also the little matter of a journal that he had been keeping, which was larded with passages in indecipherable characters, whose meaning Buschman was unable or unwilling to explain. The police believed that these coded parts related to Royal Navy ships which Buschman had been keeping under observation. As a result of this, he was charged with four offences under the Defence of the Realm Act.

The prosecution team which presented the case against Fernando Buschman at his court martial on 28 September 1915 were not at all sure that they would be able to secure a conviction. To begin with, one of the counts related to the fact that Buschman had been communicating with Flores in Holland. Unfortunately, the postal censors, not realising perhaps the implications of their actions, had withheld the letter which he had sent to the German officer. Since Heinrich Flores had never received his letter, it was a dubious proposition to assert that he and Buschman had been, in communication. It was lucky for the prosecution that when questioned, Buschman had himself mentioned the names of both Flores and Dierks and that he had received telegrams from them. At his trial, the fact that his letter had been intercepted and not forwarded to Flores passed unremarked by the defence.

Another difficulty arose from the suggestion that Flores had actually written the Brazilian passport which Buschman had been carrying. How on earth could one go about proving such a thing? Fortunately, the standard of proof required in a military court in wartime is often lower than that which would be commonly accepted in peacetime. There was no jury and those deciding on the innocence or guilt of the two men in the dock were army officers, who might reasonably be expected to have little sympathy with enemy agents, men who were spying on Britain for money. It did not take the court martial long to conclude that Fernando Buschman was guilty of espionage. His companion in the dock, one time business partner Emil Franco, was more fortunate. He was sent to prison for five years. Although the court believed that Franco had himself nothing to do with the espionage in which Buschman had been engaged, it was felt that he should have known enough to realise that he had a duty to report his partner to the authorities for the suspicious actions about which Franco knew. The execution of Fernando Buschman by firing squad was ordered to take place at the Tower of London, at 7:00 am on 19 October 1915.

On the morning of Monday, 18 October 1915, Buschman was removed from Wandsworth Barracks, where he had been detained during his trial, and taken to the Tower of London. As usual, the authorities specifically directed that the transfer from one military establishment to another must be effected with as little publicity as possible. Once he was lodged in the Tower, Fernando Buschman made an unusual request to those guarding him; that he be allowed to have his beloved violin, so that he might play it again before his death. There seemed no obvious reason for denying the condemned man this harmless favour and he was accordingly given permission to play as much as he liked in the 24 hours before he was to be shot.

Throughout that Monday night in the autumn of 1915, Fernando Buschman played all the music which he loved so much. Bach, Faure, extracts from *La Boheme* and *Tosca*; Buschman's playing filled the night before his death with haunting refrains which were audible throughout the precincts of the Tower. Indeed, he did not sleep at all that night, playing piece after piece. There was something indescribably eerie for the soldiers and Yeoman warders living at the Tower of London, to hear these melodies being produced by a man whose remaining life could be measured in hours.

At a little before seven on the morning of 19 October, the Assistant Provost arrived at Buschman's cell, with an escort of soldiers. The man who was about to die kissed his violin, before setting it down gently on the table, remarking as he did so, 'Goodbye, I shall not want you any more.'

George Breeckow: The Man Who Died of Fear

Shot at the Tower of London, 26 September 1915

In 1882 George Breeckow was born in the German town of Stettin. His father bought and sold pianos and his son joined him in this trade. George Breeckow moved to the United States in 1908 and imported pianos into that country, becoming a naturalised American citizen in 1913. The following year, his father died and Breeckow moved back to Germany to take care of his mother and sisters.

The piano business not proving as profitable as it once had, possibly due to the uncertain nature of international affairs in 1914, George Breeckow sought other employment. The outbreak of war in the summer took Breeckow by surprise and he apparently decided to leave his family to fend for themselves, bending all his efforts towards returning to the USA. With this end in mind, he applied to work as an Imperial Messenger, a member of the diplomatic corps who carries dispatches to and from embassies. Breeckow thought that this would enable him both to move back to America and also to ensure that he had a career when he got there.

Subsequent events are a little obscure, but it appears that the German Foreign Ministry told Breeckow that if he wished to work for them, then it would first be necessary for him to travel to England. There was a problem though, which was that his American passport had a Berlin stamp in it. It was explained to him that this might prejudice the British against him and that it would be better if he were to be issued with another, blank passport. Whether it really was possible for a man of Breeckow's undoubted intelligence to be so foolish is open to question, but the upshot was that he agreed to exchange his own passport for a new one, provided by German naval intelligence. This was in the name of Reginald Rowland. Having equipped their latest recruit with a false identity, Breeckow was then sent to the Hague, with instructions to contact Mr Dierks, the supposed importer and exporter of cigars.

On 11 May 1915, George Breeckow landed at Gravesend, a port in the Thames estuary. From there he made his way to London, booking into the Ivanhoe Hotel in Bloomsbury. Before leaving the Netherlands, he had been given the name of somebody whom he should get in touch with in London, a woman who was also working for Naval Intelligence. This was Louise or Lizzie Wertheim, a German who had acquired British citizenship by marrying a naturalised subject who was himself born in Germany.

Once they had met up, both Breeckow and Wertheim behaved in the most ostentatious fashion imaginable. They hired horses to ride in the royal parks of London and generally lived a most noticeable life, dining out in expensive restaurants. So keen was Lizzie Wertheim on living the high life, that she refused to travel anywhere without a maid to look after her. For two Germans to carry on in this way was bound to attract attention. Lizzie Wertheim went to Edinburgh in order to collect information about the movements of shipping in and out of the Forth, but so obvious was her interest in this subject and so persistent her questioning of, among others, naval officers, that messages were soon being sent to Special Branch regarding her activities.

It looks in retrospect as though Breeckow and Wertheim had come to some sort of agreement that she would do the actual spying and that he would then pass on the intelligence to his contacts in Holland. Almost unbelievably, the name and address to which Breeckow had been advised to send the information which he had gathered was our old friend H. Flores, at 127a Binnenweg Rotterdam. This was the same Heinrich Flores who had of course already featured in a number of spy trials. That anybody in the German intelligence services should think it a good idea to continue using this same contact is nothing short of incredible. Nevertheless, on 26 May 1915, George Breeckow duly posted several seemingly innocuous newspapers to Flores.

The package addressed to H. Flores in Rotterdam was duly intercepted and opened by the British postal censors. It came as no surprise to anybody, that a message had been written in lemon juice on one of the newspapers. This could hardly have been more incriminating, reading as it did:

Large transports of artillery on their way from Aldershot to S. The largest troop camp at present at Wareham near Swanage, but the numbers of men had decreased.

This communication, sent after Breeckow and Wertheim had visited Bournemouth, alerted Special Branch to the fact that there was another German spy on the loose.

The British had no idea where this latest spy might be found, but fortunately another letter was soon sent to the Rotterdam address. The contents of the letter were harmless enough, but every item of mail to H. Flores in Rotterdam was being closely scrutinised and when it was seen that the writer had put his own address on the back of the envelope, Inspector Herbert Finch was despatched from Scotland Yard to see who might be staying at the London hotel. Finding a German on the premises, he promptly arrested him and took him in for questioning. A few days later, Lizzie Wertheim was also brought in.

Enough was found in Breeckow's possession to make denial of his espionage activities all but impossible. Among the compromising items found in his luggage were a sheet of paper hidden in his shaving brush with details written on it of several Royal Navy vessels and the fact that he was travelling on a forged passport. One of the details that German Naval Intelligence simply could not seem to get right was the American passports which they handed out so readily to their agents. The one that George Breeckow was using, in the name of Reginald Rowland, was smaller than official American passports and the eagle was drawn incorrectly; one talon was inverted and the tail feathers were wrong. It was one of the clumsiest forgeries imaginable.

Perhaps realising that he was in a hopeless position, Breeckow decided to make a clean breast of matters and throw himself upon the court's mercy. He asked one of the police officers guarding him at Cannon Row police station, 'Am I to be tried for my life?' The officer replied that he believed that this might well happen, whereupon Breeckow asked for pen and paper and wrote a complete account of how he had come to be recruited as a spy.

Unlike the majority of the spy trials held in Britain during the First World War, the trial of George Breeckow and Louise Wertheim was held not before a court martial, but at the Old Bailey in London. The reason for this was that Wertheim was technically a British subject and so entitled to a civil trial. That being so, it was thought fairer if both she and Breeckow were tried together. Both were plainly guilty and the jury took less than ten minutes to return verdicts against them. On 17 September 1915, George Breeckow was sentenced to death by shooting and Wertheim was sent to prison for ten years.

It is likely that Breeckow had somehow persuaded himself that cooperating fully with the authorities would save his life and perhaps result in a sentence of life imprisonment, rather than death. Although everybody else in No 1 Court at the Old Bailey had expected to hear the accused man sentenced to death, it came as a dreadful shock to George Breeckow himself. He almost collapsed upon hearing the dreaded words and was unable to walk unaided from the dock. There was an appeal, but this was dismissed. The day set for the execution was 26 September.

According to contemporary accounts, the condemned man was absolutely demented with fear in the days leading up to his death. He constantly broke into fits of helpless sobbing, which caused the soldiers taking care of him to view him with a mixture of pity and disgust. On the morning of his execution, Breeckow had to be half carried to the range. Even when he had been strapped to the chair, he was still wriggling and shivering so much that it was found necessary to tighten the leather straps. This was in the interests of the man who was about to be executed, because otherwise it might have proved tricky for the members of the firing party to hit his heart.

Although everybody was anxious to get the execution over as quickly as possible, there was an unexpected delay. It was customary to bandage the eyes of those about to be shot. One or two of those executed at the Tower of London during the First World War refused this mercy; preferring to die with their eyes open and staring unafraid at those who were about to kill them. George Breeckow was a little different. He had no objection having his eyes covered, but wished this to be done with a lady's handkerchief, which he produced at the last moment. The problem was, the handkerchief was too small to fit around his head and in the end, an arrangement had to be cobbled together whereby the bandage was tied to the ends of the handkerchief, in order to make it long enough to be secured around Breeckow's head.

All the while that this was going on, the man fastened to the chair was becoming increasingly agitated and distressed. To make the task of the firing squad easier, Breeckow's shirt was unbuttoned and his bare chest exposed to view. Once his eyes were covered, the officer in charge of the proceedings tried to carry out the execution as swiftly as possible. However, before he could give the order to take aim and fire, the condemned man gave one last convulsive jerk, as though he were in the grip of some spasm. Then he apparently lost consciousness. The explanation for this was discovered by the doctor who examined the corpse after the execution. Puzzled as to why there had been so little bleeding from the bullet wounds, the doctor concluded that Breeckow's heart must actually have stopped beating before he was struck by the seven .303 bullets. In short, George Breeckow had had a

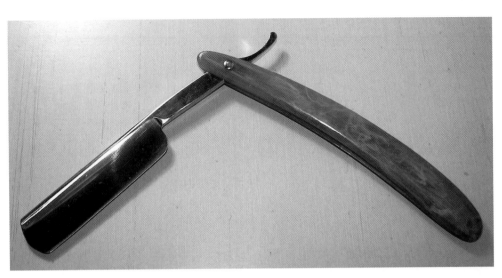

1. The open or 'cut-throat' razor; the most popular murder weapon in World War I Britain.

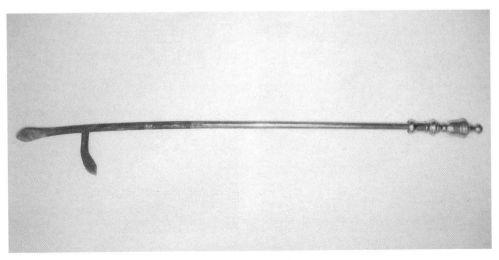

2. The fireplace poker; a fearsome weapon in the hands of an angry man or woman.

3. A 'Poker Murder', a crime which is today almost unheard of.

4. The 'Axe Murder'; another vanishingly rare crime in the modern world.

5. John Ellis, the man who hanged the majority of murderers executed in Britain during the Great War

6. Tom Pierrepoint, the other hangman at work during the First World War.

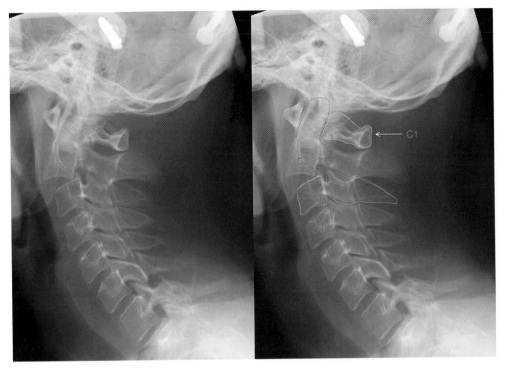

7. The classic 'hangman's fracture' which results from judicial hanging.

8. The village of Leytonstone in 1914; scene of Charles Frembd's murder of his wife.

9. The *Antillian*, the boat upon which Young Hill cut a crewmate's throat.

10. Scotland Yard today; the building from which so many murders were investigated during the First World War.

11. The indoor rifle range at the Tower of London, where eleven spies were shot.

12. Carl Lody's grave in East London.

13. Carl Lody, the first German spy to be executed in Britain, during his court martial.

14. Roger Casement, the only traitor to be hanged in Britain during the First World War.

MOTHER AND CHILD MURDERED,

SHOCKING LISCARD TRAGEDY.

NEIGHBOUR'S GHASTLY DISCOVERY.

HEADS BATTERED WITH HATCHET.

CORONER'S INQUIRY OPENED.

SENSATIONAL ARREST.

HUSBAND CHARGED WITH THE CRIMES.

15. Newspaper coverage of the 'Wallasey Hatchet Murders', which took place in Liverpool in 1917.

16. George Smith 'discovers' one of his wives in the bath.

17. George 'Brides in the Bath' Smith.

18. Bernard Spilsbury, whose work on the 'Brides in the Bath' case secured his reputation.

19. The London square where the mutilated remains of a woman were found in November 1917.

20. The scene of the 'Waterloo Road Murder' has remained unchanged for a century.

heart attack induced by his fear. He had literally died of terror and the firing squad had emptied their rifles at a man who was already dead. This was the most gruelling of the executions carried out by soldiers of the Scots Guards stationed at the Tower.

Louise Wertheim was first sent to serve her sentence at Aylesbury Prison in Buckinghamshire, but after three years there, went mad. After being certified insane, she was transferred in 1918 to Broadmoor, where she died of TB in 1920.

Eva de Bournonville: A Female Spy Sentenced to Death

Although no women were executed in Britain during the First World War, there was an interesting case of a death sentence being passed, but not carried out. This was the case of Eva de Bournonville, a Swedish governess of French origin.

In the autumn of 1915, Eva de Bournonville was down on her luck and desperate for money. She somehow came to the attention of the German intelligence services and was supplied with enough money to travel to England, where the idea was that she would gather as much information as she could about the air defences in and around the capital. A woman who she had once met and who lived in Scotland, was used as a reference when de Bournonville announced that she hoped to work for the postal censorship service. This was an exceedingly sensitive job and the friend in Scotland wrote to some people she knew in the London district of Hackney, asking that they take an interest in the lonely and penniless governess and perhaps help her in her ambitions.

After meeting Eva de Bourneville a few times, the people in Hackney to whom she had been recommended soon took alarm. She constantly asked about details of the anti-aircraft guns in London. A stream of questions came regarding the number of guns in London, their location, the height to which they could fire and so on. During a visit to Finsbury Park, de Bournonville asked if it would be possible for her new friends to show her an anti-aircraft gun site. After this, it will come as no surprise to learn that these contacts declined to act as referees for an application for a job with the postal censors. Upon being told this, Eva de Bournonville remarked menacingly that, 'The Germans know everything which passes here, you cannot hide anything from them.'

After realising that her chances of gaining a position in the censorship office were nil, Eva de Bournonville changed tack and booked into a small, private hotel in Upper Bedford Place in Bloomsbury. This establishment was very popular with officers on leave from France and the younger men were immensely flattered by the attentions which they received from the mysterious foreign-born woman. At about this time, the postal censors began to be concerned by certain letters being sent to Scandinavia. These contained snippets of gossips about military matters which, although not particularly helpful to the enemy, were detailed enough to cause alarm. Eventually, from what was said in the letters, Special Branch was able to pinpoint one hotel in London as the most likely source of the letters. This was not enough in itself, because in addition to the officers, there were thirty guests staying at the hotel.

A scheme was devised, whereby an army officer would pass on indiscrete gossip about supposedly secret weapons which were being prepared for use on the Western Front. Having selected half a dozen likely suspects, each was given details of a different, imaginary weapon. Within 48 hours, a letter was intercepted by the censors describing the very device which had been the one passed to Eva de Bournonville. Scotland Yard raided the hotel on 15 November 1915 and arrested the woman, who made no real attempt to deny what she had been up to. Indeed, it would have been hard for her to do so. What possible, innocent reason could there be for anybody to have a cake of soap impregnated with potassium ferro-cyanide? This makes marvellous invisible ink, but would hardly enhance one's complexion!

The day after her arrest, Eva de Bournonville was questioned about her activities. One of the first things which the police did was to show her the letter which she had sent to her German contact in Sweden, describing the fictitious weapon about which she had been told. The letter was in her handwriting and the invisible ink message about military matters, written between the lines of the visible writing, had been developed. There really was very little that she could say. De Bournonville was plainly taken aback to see that her private and, as she had supposed secret correspondence, was in the hands of the authorities. She exclaimed in bewilderment, 'Yes, that is my handwriting. But how did you get it?'

In addition to her invisible ink, Eva de Bournonville had in her possession a cheque for £30, which could be traced back to the German Military Attache in Sweden. It transpired that it was for this monthly wage that she had agreed to place her life in jeopardy by engaging in espionage. She made a statement to the police which admitted everything, while still attempting to put the most favourable construction upon her actions:

You may think it curious, but I always wanted to work for you and not the Germans. I am very fond of the English and the Belgians, and I do not like the Germans at all. Never have I forgotten their behaviour to Denmark. My idea was to make the Germans believe I was working for them until I was fully in their confidence and then offer my services to you. I only did this for adventure.

It was an ingenious enough explanation, but anybody sending secret messages to the enemy in time of war must surely realise that he or she is liable to end up in serious trouble. Miss de Bournville could accordingly not have been particularly surprised to find herself appearing at the Old Bailey two months later on a capital charge of espionage. On 12 January 1916, Mr Justice Darling sentenced her to death by hanging.

Even when the death penalty was in full swing and courts were sentencing people to death every week or two, there was always a marked reluctance in Britain to execute women. Consider the fact that although hundreds of men were hanged during the first half of the twentieth century, a mere sixteen women faced the supreme penalty during the same period. Between 1903 and 1923, no women at all were hanged. It was therefore thought unlikely, despite the sentence, that Eva de Bournville would in fact hang.

No sooner was Eva de Bournville lodged in Holloway Prison's condemned cell, supposedly awaiting execution, than the Home Secretary granted her a reprieve. The death sentence was commuted to imprisonment for life and she was transferred to Aylesbury to serve her sentence. The reprieved woman did not spend the rest of her life in prison. In February 1922, she was granted parole and deported back to Sweden.

Chapter Five

Suffer the Little Children:
Two Cases of Child Murder

ew crimes excite more horror and disgust than the murder of helpless children. Such offences are mercifully rare, but have always taken place from time to time. The period of the First World War saw only two such murders, both of which being what are known as 'domestic crimes'. This means that the children who died were not plucked from the streets by some roaming, homicidal maniac, but were rather killed by men who should have been exercising parental responsibility for them.

One sometimes gains the impression from the mass media that cruelty to children and the murder of children and step-children is a modern phenomenon, linked perhaps to the breakdown in traditional family structures which we have witnessed in recent years. This is not at all the case. Rare though they are, such murders have occurred from time to time throughout the whole of recorded history.

Arnold Warren: A Gambler's Last Throw

Hanged at Leicester, 12 November 1914

Being married to a gambler is sometimes a trying experience, particularly for a wife. If one is wholly reliant upon a husband's wages, then it can be dispiriting to see the money needed to pay for food and heating, vanish during a visit to the racetrack or gambling den. Ethel Mary Warren put up with this way of life rather longer than many women in her situation; she remained married to inveterate gambler Arnold for eight years and had borne him a son, before the day came when she had finally had enough. On 22 May 1914, her husband returned home and admitted that he had just hazarded the weekly housekeeping on a horse and lost the lot. This was not the first time that such a thing had happened. Despite earning good money as an engineer's fitter, 34-year-old Arnold was often completely broke. Sharp words were exchanged, feelings ran high and the upshot was that Arnold Warren lost his temper and struck Ethel round the face.

Ethel Mary Warren might have put up with gambling on horses and card games over the years, but she was not prepared to allow anyone to knock her about. She left that very day, taking with her their 2-year-old son, James. Within a few days, she had found lodgings at 2 Cromwell Cottages, in Dannet Street, Leicester. Her husband remained living at the rented house which they had occupied together, 98 Leamington Street, which was also in Leicester.

Being a single parent in 1914 was neither as easy nor as socially acceptable as is the case today. Raising a child is an expensive business and so Ethel's first step was to go to court and issue a summons against Arnold Warren for maintenance. She was awarded ten shillings a week, in modern terms 50p, which was just about enough to live on at that time. Ethel decided that if her child was to live a reasonable life, then she would have to get a job as well. She found work and Arnold Warren's mother, Mary Elizabeth Warren, agreed to look after the little boy during the day at her home at 48 Gaul Street. An 11-year-old girl called Edith Skidmore was given a small sum of money to collect James from his grandmother and take him back to his mother each evening.

Ethel Mary Warren had discovered what many wives before and since have also found out for themselves; that it is possible to forge a life for one's self even after the collapse of a profoundly unsatisfactory marriage. It was hard work, but Ethel was making a go of things with just her and her son to worry about. Whether this angered Arnold Warren, we will never know, but something about the sequence of events in the spring of 1914 caused his mind to turn eventually to murder.

At lunchtime on Friday 10 July, Ethel Warren bumped into her husband by chance beneath the clock tower at Humberstone Gate. He told her that he had given up his job in order to become a professional gambler. His latest enterprise was to stake every penny he possessed on a horse running that day at Haydock Park, a well known racecourse on Merseyside. Ominously, Arnold Warren also produced a small blue bottle which he claimed contained poison. He told his wife that if the horse, which had the promising name of Early Hope, failed to win, then it was his intention to end his life. Dramatic behaviour of this kind on the part of her husband was not altogether unknown to Ethel and so she bade him farewell and went back to work.

At 5:30 pm on that same day, Edith Skidmore collected little James from his grandmother's house and began walking home with him. It was her habit to take the child to play for a while before returning him to his mother. That evening, she took him to the Fosse Road Recreation Ground, thinking to push him on the swings for a while. In the park she came across Arnold Warren laying on the grass. They talked for a while and he asked her to take a note to his mother. She hesitated, but he assured her that he would take care of his son. Being only eleven, Edith did not know what to do for the best and in the end, she agreed to deliver the note and then come back to the park to collect her charge.

When she got to Gaul Street and Mary Warren read the note from her son, there was a certain amount of confusion. All that Arnold said in the communication as that he wished to borrow a saw. Edith Skidmore went back to Fosse Road, but Arnold Warren and his son were nowhere to be seen.

A few hours later, at 8:10 pm, Stanley Frederick Hackney and Alice Bray were walking past a piece of waste ground. Laying on the ground was what they at first took for a courting couple. When they drew closer though, they were horrified to see that one of the two figures was covered in blood. When they looked closer, they found that in fact a little boy had had his throat cut and was laying close to a man who was unconscious. It was Arnold Warren and his son James.

James Warren was dead, his throat having been neatly slashed open. Arnold Warren was taken to hospital, where he recovered. He had taken an overdose of laudanum, which is a tincture of opium in alcohol. He made a statement from his hospital bed in which he said that the horse upon which he had pinned all his hopes had failed to come in. Understandably, this had caused him to despair of his life and he had accordingly decided to end his existence, taking his son with him. Meeting Edith Skidmore with James had not been mere chance, he knew that the child often went to the playground on the way to taking his son back to his mother.

Arnold Warren's real intention was probably to hurt his wife and pay her back for leaving him. There have been several well-publicised crimes of this kind in recent years, where a vengeful ex-husband kills his children in order to punish their mother; and it is likely that Arnold Warren's crime falls into this unsavoury category. There was little to be said in Warren's defence at his trial, and on 12 November 1914, he was hanged at Leicester Prison.

Thomas McGuiness: A Cowardly Bully

Hanged at Glasgow, 18 April 1917

In 1916, a pretty young waitress caught the eye of Thomas McGuiness. The 25-year-old man was living in the Scottish city of Aberdeen and gave every impression of having fallen for Isobel Imlach, the girl who served him in the restaurant which he patronised regularly. One thing led to another and in a short time the young couple were courting. Isobel had a secret though, one which she eventually shared with a her boyfriend. Although unmarried, she had a 5-year-old son called Alexander. McGuiness told her that this made no difference to his feelings for her and he would treat the boy as his own. When he got a job in Dundee, he urged Isobel to bring her son and move to Dundee, where they could live as husband and wife.

Once the three of them were living together, Isobel Imlach soon saw another side to the quiet man with whom she had fallen in love. He began to beat her and also mistreat her beloved son. After putting up with this for a couple of months she fled to Edinburgh. Seemingly stricken with remorse, Thomas followed her there and begged to be given a second chance. What they needed, he said, was a fresh start. Why didn't the three of them all move to Glasgow, a city where nobody knew them? Foolishly, Isobel Imlach believed him and the little family all settled down in a house in Baltic Street.

Although he apparently made an effort not to beat his girlfriend so regularly, Thomas McGuiness fell into the habit of torturing her little boy instead. Little Alexander, or Alick as everybody called him, was a thin, pale and polite child. His meekness seemed to infuriate McGuiness, who devised various ways to torment him. He would twist the skin of his arms and legs so hard that he caused bruises. Even worse, he would pin the child down while puffing on a cigarette and then stub the glowing end out on the frightened boy's arms.

After they had been living at Baltic Street for a while, McGuiness decided that it was time to move and so the family relocated to Springfield Road, before settling finally at 101 Blackburn Street in Govan. In addition to brutally mistreating his girlfriend and her child, McGuiness kept them short of food. Isobel was reduced to prostitution in her efforts to scrape together enough money to feed her son.

On the morning of 8 March 1917, Isobel Imlach left the house for fifteen minutes to visit the corner shop. When she returned, it was to find little Alick sitting on McGuiness' knee, looking more dead than alive. According to Thomas McGuiness, the boy had had a fit while his mother was out and this accounted for the fact that he was blue in the face. Whether a fit would have caused the child's lips to swell up grotesquely was another matter and to Isobel, it looked as though her boyfriend had been up to his old tricks again. Snatching up little Alick, she ran with him to a neighbour. The woman took one look at the pitiful state that the child was in and offered to run and fetch a doctor. Having seen the bruises and burns which covered the child's arms, she said that she would have to get a policeman too. McGuiness, who had followed his wife to the house of the neighbour, then said that he would go at once for the doctor. He disappeared down the street.

No doctor appeared as a result of Thomas McGuiness's errand, but the one fetched by the neighbour did come, although too late to help the boy, who had died a few minutes earlier. The police turned up too and examined the frail body, dressed in pyjamas. It did not take an autopsy to reveal the ghastly abuse to which the helpless child had been subjected. His body was a mass of welts, bruises and burns. McGuiness was run to earth later that same day and arrested for the murder of Alick Imlach.

The defence team working on behalf of Thomas McGuiness faced a formidable challenge when his trial for murder opened on 24 April 1917, at the High Court in Glasgow. There was no point in denying that he had mistreated the child systematically and that this cruel behaviour had ultimately resulted in the little boy's death. Instead, the barrister representing McGuiness put all his efforts into showing that his client was insane and consequently not answerable for his actions.

Both the mother and sister of Thomas McGuiness gave evidence that he was a strange character, whose behaviour and general conduct had, from childhood, been out of the ordinary. Perhaps in order to back up these assertions, McGuiness began trembling and apparently being on the verge of having a seizure in the dock. He grimaced, swayed back and forth, mumbled to himself and generally acted as though he had lost his senses. Lord Justice Johnson, who was presiding over the trial, allowed an adjournment so that McGuiness could be given a chance to recover from his affliction. A doctor appointed by the court could find nothing the matter with him.

One difficulty for the defence was that McGuiness appeared to be perfectly able to earn a living, maintain a home and so on. If he was mad, then he had for the last 25 years managed to keep out of the asylum and somehow live a relatively normal life. Surprisingly enough, two of the jury fell for McGuiness' imposture. He was convicted of wilful murder by a majority verdict, with two of the jury wanting to find him guilty, but insane. After hearing the jury's verdict, Lord Johnstone pronounced sentence of death. The solemnity of the occasion appeared to fill McGuiness with terror and afterwards, he had to be helped down the steps to the cells.

As is not uncommon with violent bullies, Thomas McGuiness was very concerned about his own life and welfare. He went to pieces in the condemned cell and spent the three weeks before his execution in a state of near hysteria, in abject terror at the fate which awaited him. On the afternoon of Tuesday 15 May 1917, John Ellis and his assistant, Robert Baxter, knocked on the gate of Duke Street prison in Glasgow. The warders warned them that McGuiness was almost out of his mind with fear and that there might very well be problems the next morning, when they were due to hang him.

So terrified of the prospect of death was the condemned man, that he spent hours laying on his bed, simply shivering with fear of his impending death. On the morning of his execution, the prison doctor arranged for McGuiness to be offered a large glass of brandy shortly before the arrival of the hangman, in order to steady his nerves. The response was surprising and unequivocal. McGuiness declared that he had been a teetotaller his whole life long and had no intention of taking to strong liquor at this time of his life!

A minute or so before 8:00 am, Ellis and Baxter were waiting outside the condemned cell, along with the governor of the prison, the chaplain, sheriff and other officials. As the clock struck the hour, a warder opened the iron door and the hangman and his assistant entered. It was obvious that Thomas McGuiness was barely able to walk, such was his emotional state. Baxter fastened the man's hands behind his back and he was then led to the scaffold. McGuiness was scarcely able to set one foot in front of the other.

When the party reached the gallows, McGuiness was urged forward, until he was standing right beneath the beam. John Ellis produced the white cotton hood and pulled it over the prisoner's head. He then positioned the noose around McGuiness's neck. Ellis's assistant, Robert Baxter was a little slower than usual in the carrying out of his own duties and it was only now that he bent to strap the condemned man's ankles together. Ellis, in the meantime, had gone to the lever which operated the drop and, turning to look back and see if his assistant had finished securing the ankles, he noticed that the man standing there with the rope already about his neck was swaying from side to side, clearly about to faint with sheer terror. There was no time to lose and Ellis shouted for Robert Baxter to get clear at once. The assistant executioner only just managed to leap from the trapdoors before they fell.

The execution of Thomas McGuiness was one of the most stressful that John Ellis had ever undertaken. His assistant and he remembered to the end of their days, the time that the fall of the trapdoors almost sent two men, instead of one, plummeting into the pit below the gallows.

Chapter Six

The Traitor and the Spy:
Two Hangings in London

D uring the Second World War, every spy except one who was executed suffered death by hanging, with only one execution taking place by firing squad at the Tower of London. During the First World War, these proportions were precisely reversed, with every spy but one being shot at the Tower. We read the stories of some of these men in a previous chapter. It is now time to look at the story of the only spy in this country to be hanged during the First World War. Before doing so, it should be mentioned that there is still something of a mystery about this case, in that it has never been established just why this one man should have been hanged, rather than being shot. A few years after the end of the war, MI5 looked into the matter and were unable to reach any conclusion. It is likely to remain a mystery, unless at some time in the future some documents relating to the trial are declassified.

When the First World War began in 1914, it had been over 50 years since anybody had been hanged in this country for any offence other than murder. Not since Martin Doyle had been hanged at Chester in 1861, for attempted murder, had anybody suffered the supreme penalty in the United Kingdom for anything other than the wilful murder of a fellow being. Two men were hanged during the course of the war for other capital crimes. In 1915, Robert Rosenthal was hanged for espionage and the following year, Roger Casement was executed for treason in Pentonville Prison

Executions for treason have, for the last two hundred years, only taken place for acts undertaken when this country is at war. Only four men were executed for this offence in England over the course of the twentieth century; the first of whom was Roger Casement. His was the first execution for high treason for a century. It was also the only such execution to take place during the First World War. As we shall see, there was, even at the time, some doubt about the legality of the proceedings against Casement, despite the fact that he had plainly been collaborating with the Germans to assist their war effort by armed action on British territory.

Sir Roger Casement: The Disgraced Diplomat

Hanged in Pentonville, 3 August 1916

Roger Casement's story is an extraordinary one, of a man who rose very high in his nation's service, only to fall to the most abysmal depths possible. In 1911, he had been knighted for his tireless work on behalf of the mistreated natives of Africa and South America. He has been called the, 'Father of twentieth-century human rights investigations'. Five years later, he was not only reviled and executed as a traitor, but his reputation had also been blackened and besmirched. Roger Casement, it was claimed, had been the worst kind of pervert and had lived a life of shocking depravity. Seldom can there have been a more spectacular fall from grace.

On 1 September 1864, Roger Casement was born near Dublin to a Protestant father and a Catholic mother. The boy was raised as a protestant. When he left school at the age of 16, young Roger went to England to work for a shipping line. He then went to Africa, where he worked for a time in the Congo, before joining the British Colonial Service as a clerk. In 1901, he was appointed consul for the French part of the Congo. In this position, he wrote a devastating expose of the exploitation and abuse of the natives by the Belgians. A few years later, in 1906, he was sent by the Colonial Office to South America, where he also drew attention to the dreadful treatment of the natives. He was eventually promoted to the position of consul-general in Rio de Janeiro. Having already been appointed Companion of the Order of St Michael and St George in 1905, 'Congo' Casement was knighted in 1911.

In 1913, Sir Roger resigned from the Colonial Office, having become enamoured of the cause of Irish nationalism. When war was declared with Germany, Roger Casement saw that the time might have come to strike a mortal blow at the English rule of Ireland. As the old saying has it: England's misfortune is Ireland's opportunity. In August 1914, the very month that war was declared, Casement took ship for New York, where he met German diplomats and sought their aid in overthrowing the English rulers of his homeland. Two months later, he travelled to neutral Norway and from there went to Germany.

By any standard, Sir Roger Casement was skating on exceedingly thin ice. It is altogether possible that his actions, even so early in the war, could be construed as treasonous, but they were as nothing to what was to follow. For the next eighteen months, Casement was intriguing and conspiring in Germany to overthrow the English dominance of Ireland. He assured the Germans that if they would supply arms and forces to help in a revolution in Ireland, then this would divert British military forces from the Western Front. He also toured prisoner of war camps, trying to raise an 'Irish brigade' from the prisoners held in the camps. This was a miserable flop, as the soldiers held there had all willingly volunteered to fight the Germans.

The climax of Roger Casement's activities with the Germans was to negotiate the landing of 20,000 rifles on the Irish coast. The Germans refused in the end to hazard any of their own men on the expedition, but offered to land Sir Roger himself from one of their submarines. The navy intercepted the boat carrying the arms and on 21 April 1916, Roger Casement was arrested by the Royal Irish Constabulary soon after being set down on a lonely beach in County Kerry. He was at once taken to England and lodged as a prisoner in the Tower of London.

Before examining the trial of Sir Roger Casement for high treason, which began at the Old Bailey on Monday, 26 June 1916, it might be worth remembering exactly what he had done, about which there was no real dispute when he appeared in the dock. He had travelled to Germany, a country with which we were at war and then tried to seduce from their allegiance a number of British soldiers being held there. He had conspired with the enemy and urged them to send forces to Ireland to fight the Crown. Finally, he had been taken in a German U Boat to Ireland and landed there, hoping to bring with him a large consignment of weapons, which he hope would be used against the British army. For most of us, it is hard to imagine a clearer or more obvious instance of treason. Not withstanding the facts though, Casement was very nearly acquitted. To see why, we need to see why legal documents today always avoid commas and other punctuation, whenever possible.

In 1872, the United States government passed a law which was supposed to remit the duty payable on the importation of fruit-plants. By mistake, the person printing the legislation inserted a comma, rather than a hyphen, causing the law to rescind duty on, 'all fruit, plants'. This typographical error cost the government millions, until it was rectified. A very similar thing happened during Roger Casement's trial and it was sometimes asserted after his death that he had been, 'hanged on a comma'.

The law relating to treason in this country was formulated in the Treason Act of 1351 and it remains in force to this day. This was the law under which Sir Roger was charged and brought to trial. There was however a slight problem with the 1351 act; or more precisely, there were two problems. The first is that it was written in Norman French and there was, at the time of Casement's trial, no definitive translation. The second point, upon which much of the trial hinged, was that the use of commas in English was unknown until the middle of the sixteenth century, two hundred years after the Treason Act became law. This led to an ambiguity in the wording which, thought Roger Casement's lawyers, must inevitably lead to his acquittal on the charge of treason.

The charge, as read out at the beginning of the trial before the Lord Chief Justice was that Sir Roger Casement stood:

indicted and charged on the presentment of the grand jury with the following offence: High treason, by adhering to the King's enemies elsewhere than in the King's realm to wit, in the Empire of Germany contrary to the Treason Act, 1351, 25 Edward III., statute 5, chapter 2.

It was upon the interpretation of these words that a man's life or death were to be decided. There was no suggestion that Casement had committed treason or, to use the old wording, 'adhered to the King's enemies', in this country. The whole thrust of the prosecution was that his treason had been committed entirely abroad.

The case for the prosecution, presented by the Attorney General, seemed unassailable and observers at the trial were waiting with interest to see what defence Casement could possibly put forward. His counsel, Serjeant Sullivan, had only one string to his bow. But what a string it proved to be! His contention was that the charge against his client was covered by no English law and that he therefore called upon the court to dismiss the case without hearing any more evidence. It was a bold move and Viscount Reading, the Lord Chief Justice, gave Casement's defence team all the time that they needed to present their case. This is what Serjeant Sullivan said, in his opening speech:

The indictment which your lordships have before you under the new statute sets out the charge as being 'High Treason by adhering to the King's enemies elsewhere than in the King's realm,' to wit, in the Empire of Germany, contrary to the Treason Act, 1351. Now, my lords, we are all aware that that statement, in the description of the offence as far as I have gone, is certainly not taken from the words of the statute, 25 Edward III. On the contrary, the words 'elsewhere' than 'in the King's realm', so far from following the charge of adhering to the King's enemies in the statute, are followed by directly contrary words, 'adhering to the King's enemies within his realm,' and, as we all know, are followed by the further words, 'giving them aid or comfort within the realm or elsewhere,' as it has been translated.

This then was the crux of the matter. The statute under which Sir Roger Casement had been charged, made it an act of treason to 'adhere to the King's enemies within his realm'. Nobody had even hinted that Casement had done any such thing. He had associated with the King's enemies only *outside* his realm and could therefore not be convicted of treason under the 1351 Act.

If Serjeant Sullivan's move to quash the indictment was successful, then Casement would walk free from the court. It was a fascinating point and it is a tribute to the esteem in which the rule of law has always been held in this country that even in the midst of the greatest war ever known, the Lord Chief Justice was perfectly prepared to debate the question at length; even though the man on trial had so plainly been consorting with the enemy and planning to launch what was, in effect, a civil war.

Serjeant Sullivan said that the actual offence set out in the 1351 act was that:

... if a Man do levy War against our Lord the King in his Realm, or be adherent to the King's Enemies in his Realm giving to them Aid and Comfort in the Realm or elsewhere ...

then he would be guilty of treason. Sullivan's interpretation of these words was that they created two separate offences, namely levying war against the King in his realm and also adhering to the King's enemies in his realm. On that reading, Sir Roger Casement was quite innocent; none of his supposedly treasonous activities having taken place in the King's realm. The wording about giving aid and comfort to the King's enemies, 'in the realm or elsewhere' referred, according to Serjeant Sullivan, to the location of the King's enemies and not to that of the person giving the aid and comfort.

It was an ingenious defence and debating this point took up almost the whole of the three-day trial. This was not a matter for the jury to decide; the question was whether the trial should even take place under the indictment as it was framed. In the end, the Lord Chief Justice decided that had commas been in use in the fourteenth century, then the relevant wording would have read:

if a Man do levy War against our Lord the King in his Realm, or be adherent to the King's Enemies in his Realm, giving to them Aid and Comfort in the Realm, or elsewhere

In short, adhering to the King's enemies either *in* the realm or *elsewhere*, was the essence of the offence. Since there was not the slightest doubt that this was what Casement had been doing, there was little more to be said. This is why it has been said that he was hanged by a comma!

Once the ruling had been made of the meaning of that Norman French sentence, written over five hundred years earlier, there was little more to be said. No witnesses were called by the defence and Sir Roger Casement limited his evidence to giving a speech from the dock. Following this, there were closing speeches by both the prosecution and defence barristers and then the Lord Chief Justice summed up. The jury brought in a verdict of guilty and Casement was sentenced to be hanged.

There was of course an appeal, held in July before five Law Lords, here too Serjeant Sullivan's interpretation of the law was not accepted. Indeed two of the judges had taken the trouble to go to the Public Record Office and examine for themselves the original scrolls upon which the Norman French words about which they were arguing, had been first written. They told Sullivan that there were discrepancies in the wording around which the case centred. The appeal was dismissed.

So far, everything had been conducted with scrupulous and exemplary fairness. However, when a campaign began for Casement to be reprieved, the government decided that it was time to play dirty. It was not enough that Sir Roger Casement was to be hanged; they wished to see his reputation destroyed as well.

It was not generally known that Casement had for most of his adult life been a promiscuous homosexual with a *penchant* for young men whom he paid to have sex with him; today, we would perhaps say that he was addicted to rent boys. Many of these liaisons took place abroad and he kept detailed diaries in which he described frankly what he was up to. A hundred years ago, such behaviour was viewed with absolute repugnance by the average person and so the British government, who had acquired the diaries after Casement's arrest, had photographic copies made. These were circulated to potential supporters of the condemned man in both this country and also the United States. Although in later years, the story became prevalent that the diaries were forgeries produced by the British secret service, there is no reason to believe that this is the case. In fact a forensic examination ten years ago concluded that they were almost certainly genuine. It was in any case unlikely that a reprieve would have been forthcoming, but the publication of this material destroyed even the slightest hope for clemency.

Roger Casement, he had been stripped of the knighthood after his conviction, was hanged by John Ellis at London's Pentonville Prison at 9:00 am on 3 August 1916. Shortly before his execution, Casement had been received into the Catholic Church. The priest who accompanied him to his execution said afterwards that Casement was a 'saint' and that rather than praying *for* him, it would be more appropriate to pray *to* him. By all accounts, Roger Casement died bravely, marching to his death like a soldier.

Ellis, the man who hanged him, described him in later years as, 'The bravest man it ever fell to my unhappy lot to execute.'

Fifty years after his death, there was a curious coda to the life and death of Roger Casement. It had always irked the Irish state that one of its heroes and founding fathers should have been consigned to a felon's grave in an English prison and regular requests were made for the repatriation of Roger Casement's body to his native land. Finally, in 1965, this was granted and Casement's remains were sent back to Ireland, where they were accorded a state funeral. Then the rumours began. Despite the fact that a member of staff from the Irish embassy was present at the exhumation of Roger Casement's corpse, the story began to circulate in Ireland that the remains brought back from England had not been Casement's at all. It was said that the quicklime in which executed criminals were buried had completely dissolved Roger Casement's bones and that in fact the skeleton which had been brought back to Ireland and given a grand funeral had been that of the murderer Dr Crippen! The truth was somewhat worse than this and did not emerge until many years later.

In fact, the remains which were repatriated to Ireland *were* those of the famous man. In 1969, the rumours had become so widespread that an MP from Northern Ireland wrote to the Home Secretary asking about the matter. Things were so tense in the province at that time, with the 'Troubles' just beginning, that it was thought unwise to be free with the correct information. It turned out that after his execution, instructions had been sent to the prison staff at Pentonville from the government, that Casement's body was to thrown into a grave without any coffin or even a shroud and then covered in quicklime. It is thought that the idea was that the body would be rendered down and completely destroyed by this treatment, so that it could not later be exhumed. This was done with some of the leaders of the 1916 Uprising; Patrick Pearse, for example. In the event, the quicklime used at Pentonville Prison failed to dispose entirely of the corpse and the bones remained.

It was feared that if it became widely known how casually and contemptuously Casement's corpse had been treated, it might have inflamed the already volatile situation in Ulster and so the full details were not released until the early part of the present century.

Robert Rosenthal: The Spy Who was caught by Accident

Hanged at Wandsworth, 15 July 1915

There is of course an old saying to the effect that truth is stranger than fiction. In the case of Robert Rosenthal's arrest, this adage proves to be quite literally true; no writer of spy stories would dare to use as a plot the actual sequence of events which led to the capture of the third spy executed in this country during the First World War.

In a previous chapter, we looked at the trials and executions of a number of men who were convicted of spying for Germany in the early years of the war. All these men were shot by firing squads at the Tower of London. Only one spy was hanged in Britain during the First World War, for reasons which, even to this day, remain obscure.

As we have seen, the downfall of many of the spies caught in 1914 and 1915, was that they communicated quite openly by telegram or letter with German spymasters stationed in neutral countries. The British intelligence service knew most of those working for the German military and naval intelligence in other European countries and they kept a close eye on them. Mail sent from this country was routinely opened and letters to neutral countries were automatically regarded as being a little suspect. Nevertheless, one German spy operating in this country managed to avoid drawing attention to himself by the injudicious sending of telegrams to Denmark or Norway and simply set about gathering information about British naval deployments off the Scottish coast. He was remarkably successful; so successful in fact that nobody in this country guessed for a moment that he was anything other than what he claimed to be, that is to say a travelling salesman from the United States. After having collected as much intelligence as he could, this unknown spy booked a passage to Copenhagen, in order to meet up with his contact in German naval intelligence. He boarded ship in Newcastle in June 1915 and set sale for Denmark, perhaps believing himself home and dry, with his mission a resounding success.

Copenhagen was something of a centre for espionage at that time and many agents of both sides were sending letters and telegrams to and from the city. Two weeks before the man who had been spying on ships in the Firth of Forth booked his ticket to Denmark, there occurred a random accident in the sorting office of the central post office in Copenhagen. A clerk happened to slip a letter addressed to Berlin into the bag bound for England, instead of that intended for Germany.

The arrival at a British post office in 1915 of a letter addressed to an office in Berlin was certain to awaken the curiosity of anybody who saw it. In no time at all, it had been forwarded to Scotland yard's Special Branch. The letter was written in German and addressed to an officer in German naval intelligence. It made intriguing reading. The writer announced quite openly that he was about to embark on an espionage mission in England and that his cover would be that of a travelling salesman who was dealing in gas lighters. The police and intelligence service began a frantic race to find anybody who might fit this description and eventually unearthed the landing records of a young American called Robert Rosenthal, who had entered the country claiming to represent a company which was marketing a new design of patent gas lighters. Rosenthal was tracked to Newcastle and it was discovered that he was on board a ship which had just left port, heading across the North Sea to Denmark. A launch was despatched, which intercepted the ship before it had passed the three mile limit and entered international waters. It was ordered to turn back.

Basil Thompson, a detective with the Special Branch, related in his memoirs what happened next. He was given the task of interrogating 23-year-old Rosenthal when he had been brought ashore. At first, Robert Rosenthal denied everything and claimed to be an innocent American who was being outrageously detained on some trumped up accusation of spying. He certainly carried an American passport, which to Thompson's eye's looked authentic. However, he asked the man in front of him to provide a sample of his handwriting. When he had done so and it was checked against the writing in the letter addressed to Berlin, it was at once obvious that the two were identical. The police officer pointed this out to Rosenthal, whereupon the most extraordinary thing happened. Robert Rosenthal leaped to his feet, clicked his heels and announced dramatically, 'I confess everything! I am a German soldier.'

In point of fact, Robert Rosenthal was not a soldier at all, but a petty criminal enlisted by naval intelligence in Germany. The suspicion was that they had threatened him with imprisonment in order to persuade him to act as a secret agent in Britain. Robert Rosenthal had been born in Magdeburg and apprenticed as a boy to a baker in Cassel. He didn't care for the work and so returned to his home town, where he was sent to prison for three months for forgery. After being released from prison, he drifted from job to job and place to place, finding himself in Hamburg at the beginning of the war. It was here that the naval intelligence service came across him; a rootless petty criminal, living on the edge of the law.

In sharp contrast to men like Carl Lody, Rosenthal was terrified out of his wits at the prospect of being executed and tried his best to save his life by betraying his superiors in Germany. This caused those dealing with him to feel nothing but contempt for somebody who was prepared so readily to change sides. Even so, advantage was taken of the information which Rosenthal was prepared to supply. He named Fritz Prieger as the director of naval intelligence in Berlin, which the British knew to be true. What they didn't know until Rosenthal told them, was that Prieger had a limitless supply of blank American passports, with all the necessary seals and materials to make them out in any name which they wished. This explained the number of spies who had been arrested while posing as Americans.

After revealing so much to the enemy, Rosenthal was overcome with remorse and tried to strangle himself with his bedclothes. He later made a second, even more determined bid to commit suicide. After his initial interview with Basil Thompson, Rosenthal was brought to London and lodged in the guardroom at the Tower of London. Later, he was transferred to Wandsworth Barracks and then to Wandsworth Prison.

On 11 July 1915, Robert Rosenthal faced a court martial at Westminster Hall. Although he was not a soldier, under the Defence of the Realm acts which had been passed following the declaration of war, even civilians could be tried by courts martial on capital charges. The public were not admitted to the court, armed soldiers with fixed bayonets preventing anybody without official business from entering the building. The whole trial was thus held *in camera*. The evidence against the young German was damning and he had in any case confessed. All that remained was to decide on his fate. He was sentenced to death. On 15 July 1915, Thomas Pierrepoint executed Rosenthal in Wandsworth Prison.

Every other spy executed in Britain during the First World War, died in front of firing squads. Robert Rosenthal alone was hanged. This is mysterious and the real reason for his being singled out in this way has never been properly established, although there are clues. Some modern writers have claimed that Rosenthal was hanged because he was convicted by a civil, rather than a military court. This is untrue; it was a military court which tried him. In 1932, MI5 looked into the question of why Rosenthal alone of all the First World War spies was hanged and not shot. They were unable to discover a definite and unequivocal explanation. One officer to whom they spoke, a man who was involved in the case at the time, expressed the view that as a result of Rosenthal's readiness to betray information about his own side, that, 'A bullet was too good for him'. This man was disgusted at the cowardly way that Robert Rosenthal behaved during his trial. Another possible explanation was that there were administrative difficulties at the Tower of London, which made it impractical to execute him there.

The idea that it was some logistical problem involving the Tower which led to its being impossible to carry out an execution there in the middle of July that year is a convincing one. Two executions by firing squad took place on 30 July and there had already been some problems about lodging the condemned men in the Tower of London before their execution. They had arrived at the Tower on 5 June and only remained there for four days, before being transferred to the military detention barracks in Wandsworth. After a century, it is unlikely that this particular little puzzle will ever be solved, but the most probably explanation is the simplest; that there was some administrative bungle which prevented a prisoner being able to be lodged in the Tower in the middle of July 1915.

Chapter Seven

A Classic Murder Case:
George 'Brides in the Bath' Smith

Major wars seem to have a habit of overshadowing murder cases and causing them to be forgotten more quickly than those in peacetime. Most people in Britain, even sixty or seventy years later will still readily recall such famous murderers of the late 1940s and early 1950s years as Haigh, the 'Acid Bath' killer, Neville Heath, John Christie of Rillington Place, Derek Bentley and Ruth Ellis. Ask them to name a murderer from the Second World War though and they are likely to be stumped. So it is with the First World War. There were quite a few interesting and significant murder cases during the four years of war, but few people are able to remember any of them. This is perhaps understandable. The carnage on the Somme, when 20,000 young men were massacred in a single day, was bound to overshadow the killing of just one or two victims in a domestic crime.

The only British murderer from the First World War of whom anybody is likely to have heard is of course George 'Brides in the Bath' Smith. He is the first British serial killer whose name we know and for that reason alone has secured a place in forensic history. A century after his death, George Smith's life story still sounds like a work of fantastic fiction. The tale which follows serves once more to illustrate the old adage about truth being stranger than fiction. The life and crimes of George Smith were so extraordinary that they even drove from the front pages of the newspapers in 1915, news of the British offensive in the Dardanelles.

George Smith: 'I am a bit peculiar...'

Hanged at Maidstone, 13 August 1915

Since its establishment in the nineteenth century, Scotland Yard, the headquarters of the Metropolitan Police, has regularly received letters from people claiming knowledge of all manner of undetected crimes. A very large proportion of such communications are disregarded as being the work of cranks, trouble makers and the mentally unbalanced; although all are answered courteously. Once in a while though, a letter arriving at the world famous address leads to the discovery of a genuine crime.

Just before New year's Day 1915, a letter landed on the desk of Detective Superintendent John McCarthy, the man in charge of what later became known as Scotland Yard's 'murder squad'. It was from somebody called Joseph Crossley and he had seen an article in the *News of the World* on Sunday 27 December which had upset him and his wife. The headline had been, 'Bride's Death in the Bath', an account of a woman who had been married only two days, before she had tragically and unexpectedly drowned while taking a bath. What particularly struck Joseph Crossley and his wife Margaret was that precisely the same thing had happened the previous year in the boarding house which they ran in the northern seaside resort of Blackpool.

As it happened, Joseph Crossley was not the first person in the last 24 hours to have drawn Superintendent McCarthy's attention to this coincidence; if indeed it was a coincidence. The Buckinghamshire Constabulary had already been in touch about that same newspaper article. Charles Burnham, a fruit grower living in Aston Clinton in Buckinghamshire, had, like Joseph Crossley, been extremely interested to read about the tragic death of the newly married woman. It was hardly surprising that the *News of the World* article should have caught Burnham's attention; his own daughter had died in identical circumstances only a year earlier. He had contacted his solicitor, who had then passed the information on to the local police. They in turn got in touch with Scotland Yard.

The first thing that Scotland Yard needed to establish was whether there really was a link between these two tragic incidents of newly married women drowning in their baths. Coincidences do, after all, occur from time to time.

With this in mind, Superintendent McCarthy sent for one of his ablest men, Detective Chief Inspector Arthur Neil. Neil's nickname was 'Drooper', because he was round-shouldered and had a particularly lugubrious expression etched more or less permanently on his face. He was seldom seen to smile. 'Drooper' Neil was a ferociously efficient detective and soon found that the similarities between the two recently married women who had drowned in their baths were so uncanny, that coincidence could probably be ruled out at once.

Margaret Elizabeth Lofty, a clergyman's daughter, had met, and swiftly fallen in love with, a man who went by the name of John Lloyd. On 17 December 1914, less than a month after first meeting, they had been married and moved that day into rented rooms in the home of Mrs Louisa Blatch, at 14 Bismarck Road in Highgate; a district in north London. On that same day, at her new husband's insistence, Mrs Lloyd visited a Doctor Bates with her husband and complained of feeling unwell. The next day, the new Mrs Lloyd went to a solicitor and made a will which left everything to her spouse.

The day after she had made her will, just 48 hours after her wedding, was 19 December and Mrs Lloyd took a bath that evening. While she was in the bath, Mrs Blatch heard John Lloyd playing 'Nearer my God to Thee' on a small organ which she kept in the living room. A few minutes later, he went to see his landlady, telling her that he had bought some tomatoes and remarking that they would do for his wife's tea. Then he went upstairs and came down almost immediately and announced that his wife was laying dead in the bath. Because she had recently been seen by a doctor, death was assumed to be due to natural causes and following the issuing of a death certificate and a speedy inquest, the dead woman was buried on 24 December 1914.

When Chief Inspector Neil arrived at 14 Bismarck Road, he was surprised to learn that Mr Lloyd had already moved out. A few enquiries elicited the information that Margaret Lofty's life had been insured for what was then the considerable sum of £700. In modern terms, this would equate very roughly to something over £50,000. People have been murdered for a good deal less than such an amount.

It was when Drooper Neil took a train to Blackpool that things really became interesting. To begin with, there was the same breathless, whirlwind courtship. Alice Burnham, who had been 25 years of age at the time, had met the man she was to marry while they were both staying in the south coast resort of Southsea in October 1913. Alice Burnham was scraping a living at that old standby of genteel, Edwardian ladies; she was engaged as a lady's companion to an invalid. She was married on 4 November, less than a month after first meeting the man who was to become her husband. The day before the wedding took place, her soon-to-be husband had arranged for her life to be insured for £500; perhaps £40,000 in modern terms. Four days later, the lately married Mrs Smith had visited a solicitor in Southsea and made a will in her husband's favour

On 10 December, the happy couple had gone to the north of England for a holiday. They chose Blackpool. When they got off the train, they tried first to book into a guesthouse at 25 Adelaide Road, but there was no bathroom in the house, which made the place, according to Mr Smith, quite unsuitable. They had more luck with Margaret Crossley's House at 16 Regents's Road. There they secured a double room, signing in as Mr and Mrs Smith. Almost as soon as they had unpacked, Mr Smith took his wife to see a doctor. Dr Billing, of 121 Church Street South, could not find much wrong with Mrs Smith, whose husband did most of the talking and he merely prescribed her a laxative.

Three days after they arrived in Blackpool, Mr and Mrs Smith went for a walk. When they returned, Mrs Smith went upstairs to take a bath. About 15 minutes later, Mr Smith went to the kitchen, where the Crossleys were preparing dinner and left a couple of eggs, saying that they would do for breakfast the next day. Then he went upstairs and came straight down, announcing that his wife appeared to be dead.

Examining the two incidents of drowning in the bath, Neil saw that there were so many similarities that it would be all but impossible for there to be no connection between the two deaths: both were separated in time by only a year; both had been preceded by lightning courtships and swift weddings; both women had been taken to a doctor only a day or two before they drowned; both women had been insured for substantial sums of money; both had made wills about the time of their marriage; both deaths had occurred within three days of beginning a stay in a house, when there were witnesses present in the house; and there was even the same mentioning of foodstuffs that had been bought. The only difference was in the name of the man who had married the two women. It did not take long to gather descriptions which indicated that John Lloyd and George Joseph Smith were one and the same person.

After he had returned to the capital, Drooper Neil's first move was to visit the Criminal Records Bureau and see if there was anything on either John Lloyd or George Smith. He drew a blank with Lloyd, but struck gold with George Joseph Smith, whose year of birth given on his marriage certificate was 1872. George Smith had in the past been very well known to the police, although he had succeeded in keeping out of trouble for some years.

George Smith had been born in Bow, a rough part of London, in 1872. At the age of nine, he had been in trouble with the police so often, that he was sent to a reformatory in Gravesend, where he was to spend the next seven years. After his release, when he was 16, he continued his career of petty crime where he had left off, being sent to prison for six months for the theft of a bicycle. Showing remarkable prescience, his mother remarked to a friend that her son, 'would die with his boots on'. After a few more brushes with the law, Smith joined the Army. The three years which he spent with the Colours did not have a noticeable effect upon George Smith's character, because as soon as he was discharged, he began stealing again. In July 1896, he received a year's imprisonment for larceny and receiving stolen goods.

After he was released from prison, George Smith set himself up as a baker in Leicester. He ran this business under the name of Oliver Love and it was as Oliver Love that he married his first, and only legal, wife. Caroline Batrice Thornhill's family were horrified when they were introduced to the course, vulgar petty criminal from East End, whom their daughter said that she wished to marry. They boycotted the wedding, which was held on 17 January 1898. Judging by external appearance alone, it looked as though 24-year-old Smith was at last settling down and making an honest living. This was very far from being the case as in fact his criminal career had barely begun.

The newly married couple moved from Leicester to Nottingham, from there to Brighton and then finally to Hastings. This regular migration from town to town was to become something of a habit with George Smith over the next fifteen years or so. In Hastings, he forged references for his wife, which enabled her to gain a succession of positions as a maid. Acting at

Smith's instigation, she stole from all her employers, handing the proceeds of her thefts over to her husband. When she was finally caught, George Smith promptly abandoned her and moved back to London, where he undertook the first of his bigamous marriages.

It is hardly surprising that Caroline Smith felt exceedingly bitter at being used and then betrayed in such a cold blooded and calculating fashion. After she was released from prison in 1900, she moved to London and it was there that she glimpsed her husband walking down Oxford Street. He looked as though he was doing very well for himself and she was so enraged, that she found a policeman and told him that her husband was a wanted man. On 9 January 1901, George Smith was sent to prison for two years for receiving stolen goods.

Many men have false starts in their career, before finally finding their niche in life. So it was with George Smith; and when he was released from prison in 1903, he had decided that preying on women was what he was best at.

Chief Inspector Neil was able to follow Smith's criminal record only as far as 1903. There was a gap of ten years to be filled in and he set to work on this. Neil had not the slightest doubt that George Smith had killed at least two women and he arranged for the man to watched and shadowed by detectives in the London borough of Hammersmith, where he had moved after the death of his latest 'wife'. It was Drooper Neil's intention to leave George Smith at liberty for as long as necessary, so that he could gather more information about his suspect. There would be no difficulty about arresting him whenever the time was ripe, because if nothing else, Smith had certainly made false declarations in order to marry twice while he still had a living wife. He was guilty of bigamy and this might, when Neil was ready to strike, provide a handy holding charge.

Even before he had begun delving into the missing ten years in George Smith's life, Neil had uncovered enough to see what a callous, unfeeling and ruthless man he was dealing with. The speed with which Margaret Lofty had been despatched told him that. From wedding day to funeral had taken just seven days! There were other indications as to Smith's character, which were to be seen in in his conduct towards the families of the women he had married. Charles Burnham, for instance, had received a number of letters from Smith after marrying his daughter Alice. Fortunately, he had kept them and they provided an insight into Smith's nature.

Alice Burnham's father had, before she picked up with George Smith, made his daughter a gift of a little over £100. He looked after this money for his daughter, investing it at 3 per cent. As soon as Smith had married Alice, he had written to her father demanding that this money be handed over at once to Alice. In retrospect, one can see why he was in a hurry. Once the wedding had taken place on 4 November 1913, Alice Burnham had only five weeks left to live. Mr Burnham was reluctant to hand over the money at once, which caused George Smith to write and tell him that he was ruining his daughter's life. The letter ended with a threat of legal action unless the £100 was received that week. Charles Burnham responded by asking Smith about his background; trying to gauge what sort of a man it was who had married his daughter and immediately began threatening to sue his new father-in-law. Smith's reply was as follows:

> My mother was a bus horse, my father was a cab driver and my sister a rough rider over the arctic regions. My brothers were all gallant sailors on a steamroller. This is the only information I can give to those who are not entitled to ask such questions. Your despised son-in-law, Geo. J. Smith.

George Smith arranged the cheapest possible funeral for Alice Burnham after her death and did not even notify her family of either the holding of the inquest or the date of the funeral.

Margaret Crossley and her husband had been scandalised at Smith's behaviour after his wife's death. One of his first acts was to remove her wedding ring, so ensuring that it was not buried with her. This and the pauper's funeral he arranged, made such a strong impression upon the Crossleys that Margaret Crossley wrote in the visitors' book after he had left, 'George Smith. Wife died in the bath. I shall see him again some day'.

Even after his first, cursory investigation into the deaths of the two women, Chief Inspector Neil had formed the impression that he was on the track of a very grasping and cold blooded individual. He had no idea at this stage just what this man was capable of. Having demonstrated to his superior at the Yard, Superintendent McCarthy, that George Smith had murdered at least two people, Drooper Neil set off on an epic odyssey across England, piecing together George Joseph Smith's life in those ten years between being released from prison in 1903 and marrying Alice Burnham in 1913. It was an expedition which was to lead to Neil making enquiries in forty-five towns and statements being taken from over 150 witnesses. It would be tedious to recount every step in the painstaking investigation and so we shall look only at the salient points which Neil brought to light, including his discovery of a third murder.

As far as could be established, after he had left prison for the last time, George Smith devoted himself full time to preying on vulnerable women and depriving them of their money. Sometimes he 'married' them; at other times it was possible to persuade them to hand over their savings and belongings without actually going through a sham wedding.

One of the great mysteries about the case of George Smith is the way in which women apparently fell for him within days or even hours of meeting him. He was a rough, uncouth man, with no education, and yet he found no difficulty in persuading middle-class women to trust him implicitly and agree to anything which he suggested. Florence Wilson, for instance, was a middle-aged widow living in Worthing. Smith proposed to her the day after they met and, astonishingly, she at once agreed to marry him. The couple travelled up to London, where George Smith persuaded Florence to withdraw all her savings from the Post Office and give the money to him, so that he could invest it on her behalf. On 3 July 1908, Smith caught a train to Bristol, where he set up an antique shop on the proceeds of his latest swindle.

Shortly after moving to Bristol, George Smith advertised for a housekeeper. Edith Mabel Pegler was engaged for the job and soon became Smith's next wife. It seems likely that Edith Pegler was truly the love of George Smith's life, because she had no money and yet he remained with her for the next six years. This did not mean that he had given up exploiting lonely women and depriving them of their money. It was simply that after these escapades, he always returned home to Pegler. He explained his absences, some of which lasted for two or three months at a time, by pretending that he was going on business trips to Canada or Spain. When he returned, hundreds or thousands of pounds richer, he always had a story about some audacious coup which he had pulled off in the antiques or fine art business; some rare Chinese statues or a recently discovered painting by Turner, for example.

In October 1909, George Smith married again, this time to Sarah Freeman. The courtship, which took place in the port city of Southampton, was a protracted one for Smith; it took fully three weeks to get his bride to the altar. Once married, Smith, who was using the name of George Rose, took his latest wife to London. He then managed to get her to withdraw all her savings in cash and hand them over to him. In addition to this £350, he took charge of her jewellery, which he promised to have valued, worth another £200 to him. Then, during a visit to the National Gallery in London, Smith excused himself for a moment and raced back to the hotel room where he and Sarah were staying. He stole all her clothes, which fetched £100. Having made the not inconsiderable sum of £650, he went home to Edith Pegler, explaining his new wealth by telling her a story about a rare painting which he had picked up at an auction and then sold for a great profit.

To get some idea of the amounts of money that George Smith was making in this way, we must remember that a good wage for a working man at this time might be perhaps £1 a week. In other words, the proceeds from his marriage to Florence Wilson would have taken over ten years to acquire by honest labour. All that he had needed to do to get his hands on this large sum of money was make love to a lonely and vulnerable woman for a few weeks.

Some of the windfall from his marriage to Sarah Freeman Smith was invested in bricks and mortar. He bought two houses, one at 22 Glenmore Street in Southend, where he installed Edith Pegler, and another at 86 Ashley Down Road in Bristol.

It is unlikely that anybody will ever know how many women George Smith had at that point in his life robbed or otherwise exploited. Chief Inspector Neil found records of seven marriages, but there may well have been more. Smith did not always find it necessary to marry a woman in order to separate her from her money. Nor are we likely to know at what point Smith first thought of murder as a way of advancing his interests.

In the summer of 1910, George Smith married once more, this time to 31-year-old Bessie Mundy. This time, he used the name Henry Williams. The woman's chief attraction was that she possessed £2,500 and this marriage promised to be the most lucrative which he had ever undertaken. It was not until the wedding had taken place on 26 August 1910, that a frustrating and seemingly insurmountable obstacle presented itself. Bessie Mundy's money had been left to her by her father and it was held in a trust, managed by her brother and uncle. She drew an income of £8 a month, but there was no way at all that she was able to withdraw the capital. Both the uncle and brother were very suspicious of George Smith and believed, quite rightly, that he had only married Bessie for her money.

Bessie Mundy lived frugally and over the years a surplus of £130 had built up in her bank account from the income which she was receiving. It was better than nothing and so Smith got her to hand over the money and then simply abandoned her. Not only did he walk out on her, he also left behind an abusive letter in which he accused her of infecting him with a sexually transmitted disease!

Losing the £2,500 on which he had set his heart must have been a bitter blow to George Smith, but he continued singling out women and cheating them of small sums; certainly enough to provide him and Edith Pegler with a reasonable living. The thought of that £2,500 would not leave him though and he eventually worked out a way of getting his hands on it.

In March 1912, Bessie Mundy was staying in Weston-super-Mare, when whom should she bump into but 'Henry Williams', her husband. It says something about Smith's astonishing power over women that even having been abandoned in the most insulting and humiliating way imaginable, his 'wife' at once forgave him and agreed to give their marriage another chance. Indeed, extraordinary to relate, Bessie Mundy had gone shopping on 14 March and met George Smith on the way home. That very afternoon, they went together to a solicitor, who then wrote to Bessie's brother, telling him that a reconciliation had taken place and the couple would now be living together as man and wife. Two months later, they moved to the Kent resort of Herne Bay, where Smith rented a house at 80 High Street.

The only way that the £2,500 on which George Smith had set his sights could come to him was if it was left to him in his wife's will and she then died. Once he had all the pieces in place, Smith moved with astounding rapidity to execute his scheme. The house where they were living had no bathroom, which was not uncommon a hundred years ago. On 6 July 1912, George Smith visited an ironmonger, where he saw a zinc bath on offer for £2. It had no taps and would need to be filled by buckets. He managed to haggle down the price by two shillings and sixpence and had the bath delivered to his home on 9 July. The day before the bath arrived, the couple went to a local solicitor and swore out joint wills, each leaving all their property to the other in the event of death. On 10 July, Smith took his wife to see a Dr French, telling him that she had had a fit. Her husband did all the talking and Bessie just agreed with anything he told the doctor. A sedative was prescribed. Two days later, Dr French called at their home and found Mrs Williams, as he knew her, in bed. He gave her another sedative. The following morning, Saturday 13 July, a note was sent to the surgery by George Smith saying, 'Do come at once. I am afraid my wife is dead'.

When Dr French came to the house, he found Bessie laying dead in the bath, with her head under the water. Because he had seen the dead woman twice in recent days and believed her to be subject to fits, he agreed to give evidence accordingly at the inquest which would have to be held. George Smith wrote a short letter to Herbert Mundy, Bessie's brother, telling him that his sister was dead. Herbert Mundy was horrified and deeply suspicious at the news and lost no time in writing to the Coroner, suggesting a post mortem and asking him to look closely into the unexpected death.

The coroner took no notice of the letter from Herbert Mundy and after the widow and the dead woman's doctor had given their evidence, a verdict was given of 'death from misadventure from drowning from some fit'. Although Bessie Mundy's family at first opposed the granting of probate to Smith for the will which left him free to inherit the £2,500, they later withdrew their objection.

Within a very short time, George Smith had given up the house in Herne Bay and arranged for Edith Pegler to join him in nearby Margate. Even the bath was sold back to the ironmonger from whom it had been bought!

The year after Bessie Mundy's death in 1912, came that of Alice Burnham. Then in 1914, before he married Margaret Lofty, George Smith met a domestic servant called Alice Reavil. They met on 17 September 1914 and were married a fortnight later. She had been very careful with her wages and managed to save £90. As soon as they were married, Smith convinced her that the best thing she could would be to draw the whole of the money out of her Post Office savings account and let him use it to open an antique shop.

Then he disappeared with the money and also her luggage, which contained all her belongings. These were worth another £50 and so Smith walked away £140 better off for just two weeks of courtship.

The investigations being undertaken by Chief Inspector Neil were of course quite unknown to George Smith, who was now living once more with Edith Pegler, the woman to whom he always returned. On 4 January 1915, Smith visited his solicitor, Mr Davies of 60 Uxbridge Road, and asked him to try and prove Margaret Lofty's will and collect the money from the insurance company as quickly as possible.

After a month's hard work, Drooper Neil had a conference with his boss at Scotland Yard to review the evidence that they had so far accumulated. Neither Neil nor Superintendent McCarthy had the least doubt that George Joseph Smith had murdered three women. However, their suspicions were not enough. If they were to prove murder in a court of law, then they would need to have the bodies of the three women exhumed and examined by a pathologist. The problem was that if they took this step while Smith was still free, then he might very well vanish, possibly abroad. They decided that there was plenty of evidence on which to detain him on other charges.

On 1 February, George Smith breezed into his solicitor's office, only to find Chief Inspector Neil waiting for him. It must have been a nasty moment for Smith and one can imagine his relief when the Scotland Yard detective told him that he was being arrested on suspicion of making a false declaration during a marriage ceremony. Smith's relief was to be short lived. Three days after his arrest, on Thursday 4 February, the following brief item appeared in *The Times*, under the headline 'The Drowned Brides, Bodies to be Exhumed':

The Home Secretary has granted the necessary authority for the exhumation of the bodies of the two wives of John Lloyd, alias Smith, who was on Tuesday charged at Bow Street Police Court with making a false entry in his last marriage certificate.

The date of exhumation will be kept strictly private. It is understood the bodies will be examined by the Home Office experts.

Among the 'Home Office experts' referred to in the newspaper article was a still relatively unknown pathologist who had appeared for the Crown in the prosecution of Dr Crippen. His name was Bernard Spilsbury.

The case against George Smith was, at this point, far from satisfactory. It is true that the police were utterly convinced that Smith had callously drowned three women in their baths, but the question everybody was asking was: how had he done so? It will be recalled that he appeared shortly before the women were found drowned and that his window of opportunity in two of the cases, that of Alice Burnham and Margaret Lofty, was very slim. He had been seen by those present in the house and then a few seconds later had announced that he had found the women dead. Surely, drowning a fully grown woman in a small bathtub would be a long, protracted and messy business?

Not only did he examine the exhumed corpses with great care, Bernard Spilsbury also conducted some meticulous experiments with live subjects. While all this was going on, Smith was being held on remand in prison on various charges relating to his six bigamous marriages. It was not until two months after the exhumations, when Spilsbury had demonstrated his conclusions to both the Home Office and police, that George Joseph Smith was finally charged with three counts of murder, relating to Bessie Mundy, Alice Burnham and Margaret Lofty.

As is usual in cases where more than one murder is alleged, the prosecution proceeded on only one of the counts. This is so that if the first trial results in acquital, it will be possible to proceed with the other death. On Tuesday, 22 June 1915, George Joseph Smith appeared in the dock at the Central Criminal Court in London, more commonly known as the Old Bailey, and charged as follows:

That you, on the 13th day of July, in the year 1912, feloniously, wilfully and of your malice aforethought, did kill and murder Bessie Constance Annie Mundy.

A plea of 'Not guilty' was entered and the trial began under the watchful eye of Mr Justice Scrutton. Defending the prisoner was perhaps the foremost advocate of the day, Edward Marshall Hall KC.

As the prosecution outlined their case, it became clear to everybody in the court that George Smith was a particularly unpleasant individual. Before marrying Bessie Mundy, he had taken her to a solicitor and arranged to order a copy of her father's will. His aim was to try and override the provisions of the trust fund which had been set up and see if it would be possible for the woman he was about to marry to gain direct access to the £2,500 which he had his eyes on. When this proved possible, he waited until after the wedding and then tried a different solicitor. When he found that it was legally impossible to get around the safeguards of the trust fund, he simply walked out of the home he shared with his supposed wife and left town without even bidding her farewell.

The letter which Smith sent Bessie Mundy after he had deserted her was read out in court and the contents shocked everybody present. George Smith began by telling his bride that she had infected him with VD and that as a result he had to go to London for treatment. As will be remembered, he had taken with him £130 of her money, which had accumulated over the last year or two from the monthly income she received. It was plain that George Smith was worried that either her brother or uncle would set the police on his trail and so he instructed his poor bride in great detail what she should tell everybody in order to explain the absence of the money. He told her that she must say that she fell asleep on the beach and woke up to find the money missing. If she did not do this, he said, the result would be disgrace, ruin and a police case against her own relatives.

The sheer malice of George Smith's conduct did not bode well for his defence. However, being a despicable swindler who preys on lone, vulnerable women and cheats them out of their money might be one of the nastiest types of crime; but it did not carry the death penalty. It was at this point that counsel for the prosecution asked the judge if they might introduce the circumstances from the other two deaths in evidence; the aim being to show a pattern of behaviour. Smith's barrister, the formidable Marshall Hall fought tooth and nail against this, as he knew that it would very likely mean the death of his client. The jury were removed during the complex legal wrangling which then took place. In the end, Mr Justice Scrutton ruled that the other deaths could be introduced and the jury invited to see similarities between all three of the deaths.

This was the first great blow for the defence. Another was to follow shortly. It was the evidence of Bernard Spilsbury, in which he explained the sheer improbability of an accidental drowning in the bathtubs in the case and would also undertake to demonstrate to the jury just how the three women could have died.

The great problem which lay at the centre of what came to me know as the 'Brides in the Bath' case, was that it was, on the face of it, all but impossible to drown a healthy person in a few inches of water, without fierce struggles and a great deal of fighting and splashing. Spilsbury had himself carried out a number of experiments in which nurses had changed into bathing costumes and allowed the pathologist to try and drown them by holding them under water in a bath. It had proved quite impossible to hold a violently struggling person under the water long enough to cause any harm. This was the case even when Spilsbury tried to exert all his strength. It simply was not possible to use enough of a man's strength while leaning over in that awkward way. This was especially so with the baths in which Smith's victims had died. They were narrow, short and high sided.

The cramped nature of the baths also ruled out the possibility of accidental drowning through fainting or fits. Anybody passing out in one of those baths would remain sitting upright. This was of course something that the doctors and coroners might have been expected to notice.

The first thing that Bernard Spilsbury showed was that Bessie Mundy, the woman for whose murder Smith was on trial, had almost certainly died very suddenly and not through a fit or by fainting and slipping beneath the surface of the water. There were two pieces of evidence which tended towards this conclusion. The first was that when seen by the doctor shortly after death, the woman was still grasping the soap in her cold fingers. Spilsbury explained that if a person fainted while holding onto something, then their fingers would relax when they lost consciousness. In the same way, despite initially clenching during the early stage of a fit, muscles relaxed after a few seconds and anything being grasped would then be released.

Having disposed of the idea that Bessie Mundy might have suffered a fit or fainted, the pathologist went on to explain that if a person died very suddenly while holding on to an object, then the rigor mortis could cause them to retain their grip even after death.

The second reason to suppose that Bessie Mundy died very quickly was that when her exhumed body had been examined by the pathologists working for the Home Office, they discovered that gooseflesh was still visible on her arms. This too suggested sudden and rapid death.

It was now time for Bernard Spilsbury's *piece de resistance* and, once again, Edward Marshall-Hall objected and asked the judge to disallow this evidence. He was over-ruled by the judge and Spilsbury was able to show precisely how it was possible to kill a healthy person in just a few inches of bath water, without any struggling or fighting. The judge, jury and barristers retired to a room in the Old Bailey where a bath of similar dimensions to those in which Smith's 'wives' had died. This was filled with water and a nurse dressed modestly in a bathing costume then lowered herself into the water. Just as Bernard Spilsbury had said, if this young woman relaxed or even fell asleep, there simply was not enough room for her to slide down and drown. He then showed how the thing could be accomplished. Leaning over the bath, he hooked his arm under the woman's knees and yanked her legs up and out of the water. At once, her head slipped below the surface.

The results of this masterly piece of forensic deduction were even more spectacular than anybody could have expected, because the nurse promptly passed out and had to be revived with artificial respiration. It was a truly brilliant *coup de theatre* and left no doubt in anybody's mind that it was quite possible to render a person helpless immediately and cause them to die in a minute or so by use of this method.

Even Marshall Hall was reluctantly impressed by Spilsbury's careful evidence. The doctor never once allowed himself to exaggerate or go beyond what he believed to be strictly true. Indeed, his cautious answers to cross examination by the defence brought about the only laughter heard during the trial. After Bernard Spilsbury had once again declined to be drawn into speculation, by guardedly answering, 'Not necessarily' to various hypothetical questions posed by the defence, Mr Justice Scrutton remarked, 'Some day I should like to have an Act of Parliament by which witnesses who say "Not necessarily" shall be shot'. There was laughter and Edward Marshall Hall responded, 'I know other people I should like to have shot, not necessarily in this court, but in another building to which I occasionally go.' This remark also caused a burst of laughter, with even the man in the dock smiling.

Both during the commital proceedings at Bow Street magistrates' court and even now, when he was on trial for his life, George Smith kept interrupting from the dock and hurling abuse at witnesses. When Chief Inspector Neil was called to give evidence, Smith leaped to his feet and shouted that the officer was a scoundrel. The judge told him, 'You had better sit down, prisoner. You are not doing yourself any good by these interruptions'.

When the prosecution had completed their case and called all their witnesses, Smith's counsel announced that they would not be calling any evidence. Little good it would have done, because the net was woven so tightly about the man in the dock that the verdict was not much more than a formality. Edward Marshall Hall's closing speech for the defence was competent enough, but he had very little solid material with which to work.

The judge's summing up was interrupted a number of times from the dock. Realising that the summing up was unfavourable to him, Smith remarked loudly, 'You'll have me hung, the way you're going on.' A few minutes later, he said, 'Sentence me and have done with it', then 'You can go on forever, but you can't manufacture me into a murderer. I have done no murder.' Mr Justice Scrutton ignored the prisoner in the dock and continued speaking as though he had not heard him. When George Smith said, 'You would believe me just as much in the dock as in the witness box!', the judge replied quietly, 'It is just possible that that remark is accurate.' Finally, as the judge was nearing the end of his speech, Smith made one of the most famous interruptions ever heard at the Old Bailey, saying, 'It is a disgrace to a Christian country. I am not a murderer, though I am a bit peculiar.'

The jury retired for just 18 minutes before bringing in their verdict of guilty, following which Mr Justice Scrutton donned the black cap and pronounced sentence of death.

Because the murder of which he had been convicted had taken place in the Kent town of Herne Bay, the law required that it was in Kent that George Smith should be executed. He had been on remand in Pentonville prison during the trial, but after sentencing, he was transferred to Maidstone prison and lodged in the condemned cell there. His appeal was dismissed and the date for his execution set for 13 August 1915.

John Ellis arrived at Maidstone prison on the afternoon of 12 August. The governor of Maidstone was in France, where his son had been wounded and the deputy governer of Liverpool prison had taken over. He told the hangman that Smith was very depressed and that he was afraid that there might be trouble in the morning.

The newspapers had been filled with pictures of George Smith during his trial and in every one of them he had looked handsome and faultlessly turned out. His appearance was very different now. When Ellis watched the condemned man walking around the exercise yard, he thought that he looked more like a man of 63, rather than his actual age of 43. His glossy black hair was now turning white and he walked in a hunched over way, as though very dispirited. Considering that he knew he was to die in twelve hours, this is perhaps not altogether surprising.

Talking that evening with warders who had been watching over Smith, the hangman learned that the condemned man had been confirmed into the Church of England just a few days earlier, by the Bishop of Croydon. The bishop had asked Smith if he had anything to say regarding the crime for which he was soon to die, but Smith replied that he was wholly innocent. It is curious to note that George Smith was very fond of referring to God and his Christian faith, even when he was in the very process of committing murder. Shortly after his last murder, that of Margaret Lofty, he was of course famously known to have been playing hymns on an organ. His letters too, often contained appeals to God. When he resumed his marriage to Bessie Mundy in March 1912, he wrote reproachfully to her brother, saying:

Many people would rather stir up strife than make peace... I intend to be not only a true husband, but to finally make my peace, step by step, with all those who have been kind to Bessie. Why, in the name of Heaven and Christianity, should people stir up trouble when it would be more honourable to do their best to make peace?

After the death of his 'wife', George Smith wrote to her brother again, forgiving him and explaining that he was finding his own consolation in religion:

The only comforter I have now is the great God Himself, to whom I pray, and on whom I rely for sufficient strength to meet this calamity.

It really seems possible that Smith had persuaded himself that he was an innocent man, being persecuted for nothing. Certainly, there was no sign at any time of his admitting to having behaved in any way other than that of a loving husband. He maintained his innocence even when there was no hope for a reprieve and he knew that he would be going to the gallows.

George Smith showed an apparently genuine concern for the woman to whom he had returned again and again, in between his swindling and murders, Edith Pegler. He refused to allow her to visit him before his execution, because he thought that the experience would be too distressing for her. He told the warders that the legal costs of his defence had come to £1,400 in total, but that despite this, £150 remained of his savings. He had bequeathed this money to Miss Pegler.

John Ellis had a surprise when he met the assistant engaged for the execution. This was a man called Edward Taylor and Ellis found that he already knew him. One of Ellis's hobbies was keeping bulldogs and to his amazement, Edward Taylor had sold him his first bulldog, several years previously. The two of them had a lot to talk about while they prepared the gallows, during which they allowed for a drop of six feet and eight inches.

The day of the execution dawned fine and bright. There was one possible hitch in the proceedings which was preying a little on Ellis's mind. This was that the prison doctor had confided in him that George Smith had a seriously diseased heart and his professional opinion was that it might give out at any moment. The hangman was worried that the man he was about to execute might have a heart attack on the way to the scaffold.

Smith was in very low spirits on the morning that he was due to be hanged, which is perhaps not to be wondered at. He was offered a breakfast of boiled eggs, bread and butter and tea, but hardly touched it. There was a curious mixup when the officials arrived outside the condemned cell at a few minutes before 8:00 am on that Friday morning. Although he had recently been received into the Anglican church, George Smith preferred to be accompanied to his death by a Wesleyan minister. It was the custom to leave the condemned man alone in his cell with the chaplain for a short time before the execution and when Ellis arrived at the landing outside the condemned cell, together with the governor, sheriff and so on, the chaplain heard the shuffling of their feet outside the cell. Thinking that the time had come for the procession to the gallows, he got up and led Smith out of the cell. Because there was still a minute or two until the striking of the hour, Smith was gently pushed back into the cell to wait for the correct time.

It would have been the first time since his trial that George Smith had been entirely alone and it was a strange and disconcerting experience for those waiting to escort the man to his death. After what seemed to be an interminable time, the sheriff nodded to Ellis, who entered the cell.

The condemned man was standing with his back to the executioner, who walked forward and took his wrists, in order to strap them together. Smith flinched at this, but made no other protest. Leaving his assistant to lead Smith the 30 yards to the scaffold, Ellis went on ahead, so that he would be ready and waiting, with the white hood in his hand.

As he reached the trapdoors, above which hung the noose, Smith stopped dead and declared loudly, 'I am innocent of this crime!' Ellis stepped forward and guided the man forward, until his feet were on the chalk mark which was right beneath the waiting noose. After placing the hood over his head and adjusting the noose around the unresisting man's neck, Ellis was astonished to hear Smith speak again. His last words before the lever was pulled and the trapdoors beneath George Smith's feet opened, were, 'I am innocent!'

It was uncommon for condemned men to speak when actually on the scaffold and the incident stuck in John Ellis's mind. What impressed him most was not that there might be any truth in Smith's assertion that he was being unjustly executed, but that somebody on the very brink of death could be prepared to tell such a barefaced lie as his final words.

With George Smith's death, Caroline Thornhill, his only legal wife, was free to marry again. This she did on the day following Smith's execution, when she married Tom Davies, a soldier in the Royal Engineers.

Chapter Eight

Powder and Shot:
Guns: Rare British Murder Weapons

There is no great tradition in Britain of firearms being used to commit murder. Part of the reason for this must lie in the fact that for over a hundred years, the sale of firearms in the United Kingdom has been strictly controlled. In America, where guns are freely available to an alarming extent, over two thirds of all homicides entail the shooting dead of the victim. Even when there were few restrictions upon the sale of guns, as was the case during the nineteenth and early twentieth century, murders of this sort were vanishingly rare. It might have been thought that things would be a little different during wartime, with all the thousands of guns floating about the country; but a glance at the statistics of murder during the First World War show that, even then, murderers had no appetite for using firearms. Only five murders committed in Britain between 1914 and 1918 involved guns.

It is perhaps no surprise that more than one of the fatal shootings which took place in Britain during the First World War were by soldiers, who of course had ready access to guns. In the case at which we are about to look, the weapon used was not a shotgun or pistol, the commonest of the guns in circulation, but rather a military rifle. Those who habitually handle firearms as part of their lifestyle, farmers for instance with their shotguns, are often less apt to use them for murder than those who only occasionally come into contact with such deadly weapons. It is in wartime, when large numbers of young men are suddenly given access to and training in the use of firearms that trouble can begin. This is what happened in the case at which we shall next be looking at: that of Verney Asser.

One final observation which may be made is that although rare, murders involving the use of guns have traditionally attracted the most ferocious penalties in British courts. When the death penalty was still in force, it was almost unheard of for the man or woman who used a gun to commit his or her crime to be reprieved. Ruth Ellis, the last woman to hang in the United Kingdom, was not granted a commutation of her sentence for this very reason; that she had fired a pistol wildly in a quiet London street. Every one of the five men who received the death penalty in First World War Britain for shooting their victims, was ultimately hanged for the crime.

Verney Asser: A Dubious case of Suicide

Hanged at Shepton Mallet, 5 March 1918

In the autumn of 1917, the Great War had been raging for over three years. There were many colonial troops in Britain, men who had volunteered in Canada and Australia to fight for the Empire. One such group were Australians quartered on Salisbury Plain in November 1917, where they were being instructed in the use of the Lewis machine gun. Two of their instructors were also young Australians, who were friends and also rivals in love.

Verney Asser or Hasser, was 30 years old. There is some dispute about the correct spelling of his name, but since both the Wiltshire Constabulary and *The Times* newspaper use the spelling 'Asser', rather than the 'Hasser', which is sometimes used elsewhere, it is the spelling which will be used here. Asser had been walking out with a pretty young English war widow, but had then found himself cut out by 24-year-old Joseph Durkin. Durkin had, in addition to his new English girlfriend, a fiance at home in Australia. The other soldiers in the camp understood that there was some friendly rivalry between the two men, because the young widow had at first been going out with Asser, before she transferred her affections to Joseph Durkin.

On 25 November 1917, Durkin wrote to his English girlfriend, arranging for her to come and see him at the army base on 28 November. The day before this assignation, Asser and Durkin were seen eating together in the canteen and nobody noticed anything amiss.

At 9:30 pm Asser entered the hut next to that in which he and Durkin slept. This hut was the musketry store, where ammunition and spare magazines were kept. He told the man in charge of the store, Corporal Milne, that he needed some empty magazines for a Lewis gun. Five minutes after this visit, just as Corporal Milne was getting ready for bed, there came a shot from the hut. A bullet flew through the wall, passed through the corporal's rucksack and then exited through the wall on the other side of the hut. Showing a truly astonishing lack of curiosity, Milne merely assumed that the shot had been fired accidentally. Without investigating, he climbed into bed and went to sleep.

Perhaps three quarters of an hour later, he could not be sure of the exact time, Corporal Milne was again disturbed by Verney Asser, who came into the hut and was seen to be rummaging about as though looking for something. Ten minutes after Asser left, there came the sound of another shot from his hut. Even now, Milne did not trouble to see what was going on.

At 11:00 pm that night, Verney Asser went to the Sergeant of the guard at the camp and reported that one of the men sharing his hut had shot himself. The dead man was Joseph Durkin. As soon as he inspected the scene of the supposed suicide, the sergeant was deeply suspicious. The dead man was undressed and in bed. His arms were out of the bed covers and cradling a Lee-Enfield .303 rifle. A bullet from this rifle had penetrated Durkin's left cheek and travelled through his head before exiting from his right ear. It had the passed through the rolled-up blanket he was using as a pillow and continued through the wall of the hut.

There was one very curious circumstance and that was as follows. The Lee-Enfield, the standard rifle used by British forces at that time, was not an automatic wepaon. Every time shot was fired, the spent cartridge needed to be ejected by drawing back a bolt, a procedure which requires a considerable amount of force. Ejecting the cartridge in this way was drilled into the recruits until it was second nature; as soon as one fired, the bolt was worked and the spent cartridge thrown clear. Pushing the bolt forward then fed another round from the magazine into the chamber, ready to fire. The sergeant to whom Asser had reported the death noticed immediately that the catridge had been ejected after Durkin's rifle had been fired and was laying on the floor of the hut. Obviously, a man who has just shot himself through the head will not be in any fit state to work the bolt on a rifle.

Nor was this the only odd aspect of the story as told by Verney Asser. According to his account, he had been sound asleep until awoken by a shot. On lighting a match, he saw that his friend had killed himself. The only difficulty with this was that Asser was fully dressed and his bed had not been slept in. He explained that he had been sleeping on the floor and when he jumped up and saw what had happened, he had automatically picked up the rifle which had just been used by the suicide and worked the bolt to eject the cartridge. He had, he said, done this as a reflex action. He had then got dressed before reporting the death.

There was one more point to be considered when weighing up the account of the night offered by Asser and that was that he claimed to have gone to sleep at 9:40 pm and remained asleep until woken by the shot a little over an hour later. Corporal Milne though, swore that Verney Asser had entered the hut ten minutes before the time that he heard the second shot, at a time that Asser was supposedly sound asleep.

All in all, things were looking pretty bleak for Verney Asser and when the local civilian police were notified of the incident and an inquest convened for the following day, he must reasonably have expected the possibility of his being suspected of foul play to be raised. In fact, the inquest went, from his point of view, very smoothly. He was called to give evidence and testified that Durkin had been depressed about the tangle that he had become embroiled in with regard to his fiancee in Australia and the local girl with whom he was going out. It came as a great surprise to many people when the jury brought in a verdict of suicide. At this point, Asser must have thought that the whole business was over. So it would have been, had it not been for the tenacity of a local police officer, Superintendent Scott. Scott was very sceptical of the idea that Joseph Durkin had killed himself.

In addition to the other dubious circumstances surrounding the death in the army camp, there was also a purely forensic matter. When a person is shot at close range, the exploding cordite in the cartridge will cause tatooing on the skin. This burning and blackening is known as a powder burn. Such marking is very noticeable when a gun is discharged at point blank range and diminishes with distance. There were no discernible powder marks on Joseph Durkin's face, where the bullet from the rifle had entered his cheek. The clear inference was that the muzzle of the weapon which had killed Durkin was some distance from his skin.

Superintendent Scott decided to look more deeply into Durkin's death, notwithstanding the verdict at the inquest. He bought a number of joints of mutton, the flesh of sheep reacting very similarly to human bodies when struck by bullets. He also visited the mortuary and examined the corpse of the Australian soldier. Durkin had had particularly short arms, which was interesting.

By firing a .303 rifle into the pieces of mutton which he had bought, Scott found that to recreate the bullet wound on Joseph Durkin's face, it was necessary for the muzzle of the gun to be about five inches from the skin. It was physically impossible for the dead man to have held the rifle this far from his cheek and also pulled the trigger. There was of course the faint possibility that Durkin had pulled the trigger with his toe, but of course he had been tucked up in bed with his feet covered and the rifle laying on top of the bedclothes. These inconsistancies, combined with the statement of Corporal Milne, caused Superintendent Scott to order Asser's arrest. On 3 December 1917, Verney Asser was arrested and charged with the murder of Corporal Joseph Durkin.

The murder trial which took place at Devizes on 15 January 1918 was something of a sensation in Wiltshire. The fact that the inquest had already ruled that this was a case of suicide and not murder, made it more intriguing than than most such trials. There appeared, at least before the trial, to be the very real possibility that an innocent man had been hauled into the dock.

Mr Justice Avory presided over Verney Asser's trial and he was defended by S. H. Emmanuel. It did not take long for those present to see that the defence faced several insurmountable obstacles in trying to prove the accused man innocent of the crime. In the first place, there was Asser's extraordinary and quite inexplicable action in picking up the rifle, working the bolt to eject the cartridge and then placing the gun back in the hands of the man he claimed had just shot himself. Why on earth would he have done this? Then there was the fact that he had, by his own account, not sought help immediately when he woke up and found that the man in the next bed had a bullet wound though his head. He had seemingly dressed before reporting what had happened. He had even wound his puttees, long strips of cloth, around his ankles and shins; a notoriously time-consuming and fiddly process. He had certainly been in no hurry to notify anybody of the tragic incident.

At the heart of the case lay the conflict between the testimony given by Asser and the statement made by Corporal Milne in the next hut. Asser denied having been responsible for the first shot that evening; the one at about 9:40 pm which had passed through Milne's hut. He was also adamant that he had not entered the musketry store a second time and that he had slept uninterruptedly from 9:40 until woken a little before 11:00 pm by Durkin's suicide. In his summing up, the judge told the jury that they had to choose who to believe: Verney Asser or Corporal Milne. Plainly, one of the men was not telling the truth. It was hard to see what motive Milne could possibly have for lying and in the end, the jury chose to believe him rather than Asser. They brought in a verdict of guity, following which Asser was sentenced to death.

Having run a defence that his client was completely innocent and had had nothing to do with the shooting dead of Joseph Durkin, Asser's barrister now changed tack entirely for the appeal, attempting to claim that in fact Verney Asser was insane and had not therefore been responsible for his actions. It was a bold move and Emmanuel had some fairly good grounds for his audacious gambit. So swiftly had the trial followed on from the arrest, there had not been a chance fully to investigate Verney Asser's mental state. The only document which the defence had seen about this was a military record sheet which stated that in July 1916, the man had been admitted to hospital for 'mental derangement' and that he had remained in hospital for four days. Since the end of the trial, research had uncovered the fact that the diagnosis of the hospital was that Asser was an alcoholic.

There certainly appeared on the face of it to be good reason to suppose that the man who had been sentenced to death was indeed insane. Not only had his father killed himself, but Asser had spent time in several different asylums. He also claimed to have enlisted in the navy previously, using the name 'James Nugent'. He had used a false name, he said, because he was worried that if the enlisting officer had known that he had been a resident in a lunatic asylum, he would not have allowed him to sign up. Records were found that a James Nugent had indeed enlisted as a bugler and subsequently been discharged for dementia.

There was no doubt that Verney Asser's case for being considered insane was a strong and convincing one. The appeal court though, while not denying that the evidence produced was worth considering, ruled that they had no power to examine this aspect of the case, which was not produced at the original trial. On 5 March 1918, Asser was hanged at Shepton Mallet prison.

Chapter Nine

Beating to Death:
The Most Ancient Type of Murder

Scripture tells us that Cain went into the fields with his brother Abel and then, 'Rose up against Abel his brother and slew him'. Presumably this ancient prototype for the act of murder was committed by simply battering his brother to death, either with his fists or the well-known 'blunt instrument'. Killing one's victim by striking him or her with either any convenient object which comes to hand, or even just boots or bare hands, is the most basic and primitive way of committing murder. Because most men are capable of putting up a spirited defence to an attack by one other man, murders such as this usually involve either a gang of men setting upon one man or a single man beating a woman to death.

Killing a person without a weapon or with just the first blunt object which comes to hand is not easy and so most such attempts end up as instances of assault or, at worst, grievous bodily harm; rather than murder. It takes a fairly sustained and determined attack to kill somebody just by kicking or punching. Even being belaboured with a stick or something similar is unlikely to result in death. Those killed in this way have either been subjected to a ferocious and sustained assault or have just been unlucky; perhaps a blow has caught them by chance on a vulnerable part of their body.

In this chapter, we will look at two cases of people being beaten to death; one a woman and the other a man. The man was a victim of a group attack, which made it more difficult for him to defend himself. In the case of the woman, she was a victim of what we would today call domestic violence: killed by a bullying husband.

Daniel Sullivan: The Life and Death of a Drunken Bully

Hanged at Swansea, 6 September 1916

This is a story of domestic violence; an abusive marriage which lasted for seven years, before ending in tragedy. As it still so frequently does in cases of this sort, alcohol played a part in the unhappy life led by the couple who both lost their lives as a consequence of the events which unfolded in the summer of 1916.

In 1909, Daniel Sullivan, a 29-year-old labourer from Cork, married a widow with two young children. Catherine Colbert was, like her new husband, fond of a drink and it was later suggested that this played a role in the subsequent events. In addition to the 6-year-old boy and 2-year-old girl that she already had when they married, Catherine gave birth to two more children with Sullivan. In 1913, the family of six moved to 20 Cwm-Canol Street in the Welsh village of Dowlais. It was a happy choice of address for Catherine Sullivan, for her sister Hannah lived on the opposite side of the street at number five.

Daniel Sullivan was known among the Irish community of Dowlais as 'Big Dan'. He was a burly man, who had never been known to lose a fight; of which he had had quite a few when he was 'in his cups'. Like his wife, Dan Sullivan enjoyed a drink and by the time they moved to Dowlais, both he and his wife had been convicted of being drunk and disorderly. In addition to his partiality for drink, Sullivan had another habit, which was knocking his wife about. This was more or less public knowledge; certainly Catherine's sister Hannah knew all about it. A century ago though, a husband coming home from the pub tipsy and then striking his wife because she hadn't prepared his dinner, did not raise as many eyebrows as it would today. Although her sister had advised her more than once to leave her drunken bully of a husband, Catherine stayed, because she did not know how she would have coped alone. Besides, she thought that her children needed a father.

On the morning of Saturday, 8 July 1916, Hannah saw her sister cleaning the windows at the front of her house. Big Dan Sullivan went out that morning, firstly to work a shift in the coke plant, where many of the local Irishmen worked, and then to go to the pub with his mates. At number 20, the day passed peacefully enough in Sullivan's absence until he returned home from work in the afternoon. He then went out drinking with his friends. At 7:30 that evening, his son Frederick, who was now 13, announced that he was going out to visit some friends. Daniel Sullivan had in the meantime been going from pub to pub, growing steadily more intoxicated as the afternoon passed and turned to evening.

At 8:30 pm, Sullivan arrived at the Antelope Inn, where he asked the landlord, Daniel Edwards, to sell him a bottle of rum to take home. This put Edwards in an awkward position, because the strict licensing introduced during the war mean that the sales of spirits to be drunk off the premises could technically only take place between noon and 2:30 pm. However, Sullivan was already drunk and the landlord feared an ugly scene if he should refuse. In the end, he sold a bottle of rum to the drunken man, a decision he was later to regret.

On returning home a few minutes later, Big Dan Sullivan began roaring the sort of question that one would think only a bullying husband in a cartoon might come out with. As soon as he was through the door, he shouted, 'Where's my dinner?' Unfortunately for his wife, she had cooked nothing. In fact, she was asleep with the baby in a bedroom which was in a room off the kitchen. We have the evidence of Catherine Sullivan's 9-year-old daughter Bridget as to what next happened. When he found that not only was there not a hot meal waiting for him, but that his wife was actually in bed, Sullivan went mad, shouting that, 'There will be a corpse leaving this room tonight!'

Big Dan hauled his wife from the bed and began systematically kicking her with his hobnailed boots. Little Bridget begged him not to hurt her mother, but he took no notice. At this point, Frederick came home and found his mother being mistreated to a far worse extent than he had ever seen before. It was not uncommon for Sullivan to punch and slap his wife, but never before had he launched such an attack upon her. The boy ran from the house to fetch help, knowing that he would be no match for the furious drunk who was laying into his mother so savagely. He ran first across the road to alert his aunt, but finding her out, he then went to knock on the door of another friend of his mother. She too appeared to be out. In desperation, the boy ran to the local police station and told them that he was afraid that his mother was being murdered.

When Sergeant Thomas Davies arrived at the little terrace house, he found Catherine Sullivan in a very bad way. She was covered in blood and had many cuts and bruises. The police officer enlisted the aid of two women from neighbouring houses to carry the unconscious woman to her bed. Daniel Sullivan was hopelessly drunk and didn't seem to grasp the seriousness of the situation. He told Sergeant Davies that his wife was always drunk. Other than that, he had nothing to say for himself. A doctor was summoned, but there was little that Dr Cecil Williams could do, other than make his patient as comfortable as possible. Catherine Sullivan died of her injuries at 3:00 am on the Sunday morning. Sullivan had already been charged with causing grievous bodily harm. On Sunday, he was charged with the murder of his wife.

On 11 July, Sullivan appeared before the magistrates and was remanded in custody until the next assizes were to be held at Swansea. Surprisingly, given the nature of the crime with which he was charged, there was a good deal of sympathy in Dowlais for him. A collection was made for a defence fund and it raised a considerable amount of money. A fortnight after Sullivan was remanded by the magistrates to stand trial, another man was summonsed to stand before the same bench. Daniel Edwards, licensee of the Antelope Inn, pleaded guilty to the illegal sale of spirits; for which offence he was fined.

The legal process moved with much greater celerity a century ago than is now the case. These days, we would typically expect a murder trial to take place between six and nine months after the arrest. Big Dan though was brought to trial on 22 July, a little under two weeks since he had been charged with murder.

The trial at Swansea was held before Mr Justice Ridley. There was no real dispute about the events which had taken place on 8 July and Sullivan's defence rested upon the slim possibility of the charge being bargained down to one of manslaughter, rather than murder. He was perhaps unfortunate in the judge, because Mr Justice Ridley made no secret of his feelings about the case, either during the trial or later, in his summing up.

The evidence was straightforward and unambiguous. Sergeant Davies went into the witness box and testified to finding Catherine Sullivan in her kitchen. He mentioned that he was familiar with the address, because he had been called there on a number of occasions because of violent quarrels between the couple. He also said that both had been arrested in the past for drunkenness. When charged with causing grievous bodily harm to his wife, Sullivan's only response was to say, 'I wouldn't have done it if I was not in drink.'

Dr Cecil Jones, who had attended the dead woman in her final hours, had also undertaken the post mortem. His evidence makes grim reading indeed and perhaps did more than anything else to ensure that the man in the dock would not escape justice. After dealing with various cuts and bruises to Catherine's face, Dr Jones moved on to detail the injuries which had actually killed her. He said that the anus was extensively bruised and the vulva discoloured and lacerated. He thought that the damage had probably been inflicted by repeated kicking with a heavy boot. The cause of death was shock and loss of blood; principally from the injury to the anus.

Daniel Sullivan's only defence was that he had been too drunk to know what he was doing. This is of course, for obvious reasons, no excuse in law. Sullivan had chosen to get drunk and so was ultimately responsible for the consequences of that decision. Not only that, but there was the damning statement from little Bridget Colburn, his stepdaughter. Although only nine years-old, she was allowed to give evidence at the trial and was quite certain that Daniel Sullivan had stated that, 'A corpse would leave the room.' This suggested a degree of premeditation.

It took the jury less than hour to find Sullivan guilty and when asked if had anything to say before sentence was passed, limited himself to asking, 'Can I make an appeal?' At no time, either then or later, had he expressed any remorse or even sorrow for what he had done.

The appeal was heard in London on 22 August, but by then a petition had been launched, urging the Home Secretary to grant a reprieve. Amazingly, it was signed by over 2,000 people. When Daniel Sullivan found himself before the Lord Chief Justice and two other judges, they did not waste much time on dismissing the appeal. The grounds for the appeal, that Sullivan had been too drunk to form the intention to commit murder and that there was therefore no 'malice aforethought' did not wash, in light of his stepdaughter's statement. Even after the appeal was dismissed, another petition was raised, asking for mercy, but the Home Secretary announced that there would be no reprieve. The law would take its course.

It was now that Big Dan Sullivan showed his true colours. Like so many bullies, he was a coward at heart and very concerned about his own welfare. The prospect of being hanged filled him with terror. Although he not given any indication that he was sorry for killing his wife, he was certainly very sorry that he was going to be put death for his crime.

This was the first execution that John Ellis had carried out at Swansea and he was far from satisfied with the arrangements he found in the prison. The execution chamber, almost unbelievably, doubled as a workshop for the prisoners. The prison ran a commercial business making doormats and the room where these were woven had the beam of the gallows running along the ceiling. Even more grotesquely, those working there were compelled to walk across the trapdoors of the scaffold to get from one side of the room to the other. On the days that executions took place, the machinery was cleared away and the men kept in their cells until the hanging was over.

Apart from the macabre circumstance of men being compelled to work literally in the shadow of the gallows, there was a practical problem which troubled Ellis. The trapdoors were set into a recess in the wooden floor, which was three inches lower than the rest of the floor. It was the hangman's usual practise to pull the hood over a man's head at the first opportunity, sometimes as he approached the waiting noose. With a step of this sort, there would be a danger of the condemned man stumbling or tripping. Nor was this the only difficulty that Ellis saw. The condemned cell was over a hundred yards from the scaffold. This was much further than it was in other prisons, where the execution chamber was typically right next door to the cell from which the prisoner was led to his death.

Later on that day, while John Ellis was trying to work out the best way of dealing with these two unusual aspects of the hanging which he was to undertake at 8:00 am the next day, he received a strange request. Because it was wartime, many of the warders at the prison had been conscripted and some had been replaced with women. Two of these female warders approached Ellis and asked if they might be present at the execution. It seemed that they had always wanted to see a hanging! Ellis had no objection himself and referred them to the governor. After being told that they would first need to be checked over by the doctor to see if they would stand up to such an experience, both women changed their minds. It was just one more curious incident in what the hangman had already decided was becoming one of the trickiest executions he had ever conducted.

To spare Sullivan the ordeal of walking a hundred yards to the gallows, it was decided to move him, early the next morning, to a small office near the weaving shed. That way, he would have a far shorter walk when the time came for that final walk to the gallows. Shortly before he went in to pinion the prisoner, a warder came out to see Ellis. He had in his hand, of all extraordinary things, the stub of the cigarette which Sullivan had just finished and was to be the last he ever smoked in his life. Bizarrely, John Ellis asked if he might keep this as a souvenir.

When the time came to collect Big Dan Sullivan and take him to the gallows, Ellis found that the man was in a frightful state. Although he had never shown any sorrow for the woman he had kicked to death, Sullivan was without doubt terribly upset about the fact that he was shortly going to die himself. He was crying like a child. Clutched in his hand was a handkerchief which was wringing wet with all the tears that he had shed for himself that morning. Even though there was only a short distance to walk now, Sullivan could barely keep moving, constantly stopping and stumbling, as though his legs were about to give way. It was John Ellis's opinion that if he hadn't moved very swiftly at the end to pull the hood over Sullivan's head, place the noose around his neck and dart to the lever, then Big Dan would have fainted clean away.

When, after his retirement, John Ellis wrote his reminiscences of his career as chief hangman, he remarked upon something which he had noticed time and again. This was that the worst bullies and braggarts always seemed to be the greatest cowards when the time came for them to die. This was certainly so with the other case of beating to death at which we shall now look: that of Joseph Jones, who was convicted of the Waterloo Road Murder.

Joseph Jones: The Waterloo Road Murderer

Hanged at Wandsworth, 21 February 1918

A lot of crimes that we think of as being a modern scourge have actually been around for years. Mugging, for example, dates back centuries; if not millennia. Certainly, it was being regularly practised in Britain a hundred years ago. Wartime provides many new opportunities for the commission of old crimes, soldiers on leave with a little money in their pockets being regarded as being particularly profitable targets. Rudyard Kipling refers to this in his poem *Tommy*, when he talks of, 'Hustlin' drunken soldiers when they're goin' large a bit'.

During the First World War London was full of soldiers from the colonies, chiefly Canada, Australia and New Zealand. Being far away from home, many of these men were lonely and only to happy to be befriended by those who apparently wanted their company for a night out. Such a one was Private Oliver Gilbert Imley of the 87th Battalion of the Canadian Infantry Quebec Regiment. His unit was not due to sail for France for a few days and the men had been given leave, so that they could do some sightseeing in the Capital before setting off for the slaughter of the Western Front. The regiment was stationed at Aldershot and so, with his friend and fellow soldier John McKinley, Imley caught a train from Aldershot to London, arriving at Waterloo Station on the evening of 8 November 1917.

The two young soldiers began by visiting one or two pubs near the railway station, where they fell in with a couple of fellow colonials: Australian soldiers called Ernest Sharpe and Thomas McGuire. These two men appeared to know the area well and offered to take the Canadians to somewhere that they could meet girls. At one point, two girls joined the group, along with a burly man called Joseph Jones. The girls, Hettie O'Connell and Emily Birmingham, left, and the Canadians allowed themselves to be guided along some backstreets and alleyways off Waterloo Road, on the promise of being taken to some exciting and unusual nightlife.

What neither Oliver Imley nor his friend John knew was that their companions had for a month or so been working as a team to rob innocent and unwary soldiers. Their method was always the same. The Australians, who were deserters, would chum up with one or two fellow exiles, either from their own country or, as in this case, from Canada. Then Jones would appear with a girl or two, the hint being made that there would be some sexual activity in the offing before long. Then the victim, by that time a little the worse for wear, would be led to some lonely spot and robbed.

Joseph Jones, although only 26 years-old, had already acquired an unenviable criminal record. Most of the offences for which he had been convicted involved violence and robbery. He had served in the army and been discharged for medical reasons, since when he had made a living on the edge of the law.

The party of five men walked south along Waterloo Road and then the Australians led them into some of the dingy side streets and alleys which branched off from the main road. They claimed to be heading for a cheap bar, which would be full of girls who liked a good time. When they reached a quiet, narrow lane called Valentine Place, which was lined with warehouses, the mood suddenly changed and Joseph Jones demanded money from Oliver Imley and his friend. Imley handed over a few shillings and John McKinley offered a half crown. Such modest sums were not at all what the other three men had in mind though and they began beating the Canadians viciously.

As the two men went down in a flurry of fists and boots, one of the attackers drew a wooden club from inside his coat and struck Imley a powerful blow on the back of his head. McKinley was by this time only half conscious himself and was vaguely aware of his pockets being rifled. He had £8 on him at the time, while Imley had £27. These were substantial sums of money a century ago and made the robbery well worthwhile for the men who had been beating them. Once they had taken all the Canadians' money, they ran off.

The savagery of the the attack was such that Jon McKinley was still in a wheelchair a week later. He was lucky. Oliver Imley died a few hours after being robbed.

Although the police had a shrewd idea who was behind the murder, it took them a little while to lay their hands on the men for whom they were looking. When they did so, Ernest Sharpe, aged 26, Joseph Jones, also 26 and Thomas Vincent McGuire, who was 23, were all charged with a number of offences and brought before Tower Bridge magistrates' court. There, they were remanded in custody to stand trial at the Old Bailey on charges of murder, robbery with violence and assault.

In such desperate situations as this, when men are facing the very real possibility of being hanged, it is usually a matter of time before one of them will try to save his own neck, even at the expense of his friends' lives. Ernest Sharp asked to see the detectives in charge of the case and quickly struck a deal with them. Detective Inspector Storey and Detective Sergeant

Farrant, both from Kennington Road police station, were relieved at this development. Although they were sure that they had the right men, the evidence was slight and there was a very real possibility that a jury might acquit them. It was agreed that Sharpe would turn King's Evidence in return for the dropping of the murder charge against him and that he would testify against his companions in crime.

It is worth remembering at this point that there really was nothing to choose between the three men who had been involved in the robbery and murder of Oliver Imley. They had all set out to use violence to commit robbery, as a result of which a man had died. Under the established doctrine of 'common purpose' they were all as guilty as each other. The law is quite plain on this matter. If a group of people join together to commit an offence of violence and death results, all are equally guilty of murder. However, by making the deal with Ernest Sharpe, they were certain to obtain at least one conviction for murder and so Inspector Storey reluctantly agreed to immunity for one of the gang.

On 14 January 1918, the three men appeared before Mr Justice Darling at the Old Bailey. It was now a race between the two defendants who were still charged with murder to save their own necks from the noose. Thomas McGuire decided, probably on the advice of his barrister, to admit openly that he had taken part in the robbery. He agreed that he had assaulted and robbed John McKinley, but flatly denied that he had laid a finger on the dead man. That, he claimed, was all Joseph Jones's doing. Jones had, apparently to the surprise of both Australians, produced a police truncheon and used this to batter the defenceless young soldier over the head, killing him in the process.

For his part, Jones' evidence was that he had never had a truncheon in his possession. It was a lie which weighed heavily with the jury, because witnesses were called who had seen Jones with just such a weapon shortly before the murder.

It must have been a singularly unedifying sight for those in court during this trial, watching three former friends and associates, each frantically trying to blame the others for a murder in which they were all so clearly implicated. In the end, the jury gave Thomas McGuire the benefit of an exceeding slender doubt and acquitted him of murder. He and Sharpe were convicted of robbery with violence, for which Sharpe was sentenced to seven years penal servitude and McGuire ten. Joseph Jones alone was convicted of both murder and robbery with violence. He was sentenced to death for the murder and also given ten years for the robbery itself. The judge was taking no chances on an appeal subsequently being successful and wanted to ensure that at the very least, such a violent man would spend a good length of time in prison.

Awful as his crime was, it is possible to have some sympathy for the predicament in which Jones now found himself. Three men set out to commit a violent robbery and only one of them faces the ultimate punishment. This rankling sense of injustice is evident when Jospeh Jones appealed against his conviction. His counsel's chief point was that it was unfair to send a man to the gallows solely on the word of two men who had been sent to prison for the same crime; a fair point indeed. The court did not see it in this light though and dismissed the appeal.

Jones had taken the death sentence very badly and some of the warders at Wandsworth prison thought that he might go to pieces with fear before the execution. Because the condemned cell was currently occupied by another man under sentence of death, Arthur Stamrowsky, at whose case we have already looked, Joseph Jones was temporarily lodged in the prison hospital. After Stamrosky was hanged, Jones was moved into the condemned cell to await his own execution and he became convinced that it was haunted by the ghost of the previous occupant. As a result, he did not sleep at all for the first two nights that he was there.

After his last execution at Wandsworth Prison, which took place only a week before he was due to hang Joseph Jones and which ended up with the executed man choking to death rather than having his neck broken, John Ellis was especially keen to make sure that the drop he gave was long enough. When he arrived at the prison on the afternoon of Wednesday, 20 February 1918, Ellis at once went to check the scaffold. After he had done so, but before he had fixed the rope according to the length of the drop that he would be giving the next day, Ellis found himself in conversation with the under-sheriff, Mr Metcalf. Perhaps because the last execution had not gone as smoothly as might have been hoped, Metcalf asked the hangman what drop he intended to give, reminding him that the Home Office table recommended a drop of seven feet and three inches for a man of Jones' weight.

'Well,' said Ellis thoughtfully, 'It is my experience that the doctor here believes in long drops, the same as I do.'

'Maybe,' replied Metcalf cautiously, 'But I don't want us to deviate from the Home Office scale, if we can avoid it. I want you and me to be on the safe side if anything goes wrong. But if the doctor suggests any other drop than the scale provides for, then he takes the responsibility off our shoulders.'

For John Ellis, the implication was clear. It was in the best interests of both he and the under-sheriff to make sure that any longer drop than the one found in the table should only be given with the doctor's agreement.

Try as he might, Ellis could not track down the prison doctor that evening and so he was obliged to wait until an hour or so before the execution was due to take place before fixing the drop. Before speaking to the doctor on the subject, the hangman had decided to be a little cunning in order to get his own way. When asked by the doctor what length of drop he had in mind, Ellis told the man that he was thinking of eight feet. This was nine inches more than the Home Office figure and the doctor at once said that he could not sanction such a long drop. Appearing put out, Ellis said with the appearance of reluctance, 'Well, what about seven feet and ten inches, then?' To which the doctor immediately assented. It was the drop which Ellis had wanted to give the condemned man all along.

Sometimes, the man about to be hanged will try various tricks in order to prolong his life, even by so little as an extra few seconds. Jones was a man of this type and was, according both to what the warders told him and also Ellis's own judgement, terrified out of his wits and liable to collapse unless the whole thing was carried out as quickly as possible. When he entered the cell and strapped Joseph Jones's hands behind his back, the man offered no resistance, but suddenly announced that he wished for one hand to be freed, so that he could shake hands with the warders who had been guarding him. Although one of the witnesses later accused him of being hard-hearted and unfeeling, Ellis thought that any delay would have increased the chances of Jones fainting and having to be carried to the scaffold unconscious, something which he wished to avoid at all costs.

The warders, taking their cue from Ellis, reached round behind Jones and grasped his hands that way. The procession then began to move towards the scaffold. Before they set off, the hangman said to Jones in a low voice, 'When we get there, you'll see a chalk mark on the floor. Put your feet against that and it will all be over very quickly.' In the event, there was a slight, but trifling, complication.

When they reached the gallows, Ellis pulled the hood over Joseph Jones's head, the chaplain now approaching, intoning the burial service for the dead. The man beneath the noose turned his body towards the voice reciting the prayers and Ellis, not wanting to distract the man, now that his mind seemed at last to be focused upon better things, simply followed him round and placed the noose around his neck as he turned. Just before drop fell, Jones exclaimed emphatically, 'God forgive them!'; which those present took to be a reference to the two men whose testimony had sealed his fate.

Chapter Ten

Moving Towards the Modern World: Knife Crime During the First World War

A lmost half of all murders in the United Kingdom are today committed with sharp, pointed implements; almost invariably knives. Stabbing to death with knives has become by far the most common method of homicide. Of course, murders involving stabbing have been a feature of violent crime in many parts of the world for thousands of years, but it was only with the demise of such humble and ubiquitous household tools as open razors, pokers and hatchets that the ordinary knife began to enjoy such phenomenal success as a murder weapon in the British Isles.

Perhaps the single most important factor in the increasing number of murders by stabbing was the exponential growth in the use of safety razors which took place in the Western World during the twentieth century. Until the end of the nineteenth century, men who wished to be clean shaven used an open razor. Although the safety razor made its appearance in 1901, it was slow to catch on. Sales took off astronomically when Gillette struck a deal with the US Army in 1917, as every American soldier coming to war in Europe was equipped by the army with a Gillette safety razor. These men generally became converts to the safety razor and unconsciously acted as missionaries to that end while they were stationed in Britain. From the end of the First World War, the open razor's days were definitely numbered.

This meant of course, that an angry man snatching up the first deadly weapon to hand in the average home would, as the century drew on, be increasingly unlikely to find an open razor laying around. This was all to come though during the years at which we are looking and during the war the razor ruled as far as murder went. Only four of the men executed in the years from 1914 to 1918 used knives to stab their intended victims to death. Two of those cases were run-of-the-mill domestic crimes, but there are points of interest in the other two instances. The first of these murders at which we shall look was committed by a member of one of the largest ethnic minority communities in Britain at that time: the Chinese in East London.

Lee Kun: The 'Chinese Murder Case'

Hanged at Pentonville, 1 January 1916

Courts in this country are used to hearing far-fetched and improbable explanations from those who find themselves in the dock. After all, you have to say *something* if you are accused of a crime and even a feeble and unconvincing defence is usually better than nothing. Every so often though, courts are presented with truly fantastic accounts which are intended to exculpate the defendant and persuade a jury to set them free. Seldom can a less plausible story have been told with this end in mind than that which was heard at the Old Bailey on 27 November 1915.

Clara Thomas was, by the standards prevailing in 1915, what might have been termed, a 'flighty piece of goods'. She flitted from one man to another, never staying long with any of them. Just as she changed her men more often than most women did in those days, so too did she switch names from time to time. Her given name was Clara and she had been married to a man from whom she had acquired the surname Thomas, but found that the state of matrimony did not really suit her. Not long after the wedding, she left her husband and picked up with a 26-year-old Chinese sailor called Lee Kun. It was at this time that she began to call herself Elsie Goddard.

Limehouse, down by the London docks, is of course famous as having once been London's chief area of Chinese settlement. The novels of Sax Rohmer made Limehouse famous as the haunt of that criminal mastermind, Fu Manchu. In the early part of the twentieth century, the Chinese community began to spill over from Limehouse into neighbouring Poplar, in particular one street, just off Poplar High Road, called Pennyfields. It was to Pennyfields that Clara Thomas, *alias* Elsie Goddard, moved with her new man. There were very few English girls living in Pennyfields and the fact that she was living there, unmarried, with a Chinese man caused raised eyebrows among her family and friends.

Clara's relationship with Lee Kun did not last very long and while he was away at sea, she picked up with another sailor, a Russian who was known as 'Swanny'. She moved into a house in nearby King Street with her new boyfriend; a house that they shared with a close female friend of Clara Thomas's called Harriet Wheaton. Lee Kun returned from his latest voyage to find that Clara had moved out.

Anybody in Lee Kun's position might have been a little upset at discovering that the love of his life had deserted him, but there was seemingly a little more to his distress than simply the loss of a girlfriend. According to Lee Kun, Clara had been making free with his money while he was gone and he wanted it back. On 10 October 1915, the Chinese sailor went round to the house in King Street where Clara Thomas was now living and spoke quite sharply to the Russian called Swanny. He explained the situation to him and asked for his money back. Whether because of a language problem or for other reasons, Lee Kun left empty handed. According to a local landlord called William Fossard, Clara's dissatisfied former lover then went to the local police station to lay a complaint, but was not taken seriously. His English was far from fluent and so he asked a friend of his whose command of English vernacular was better than his own to visit Clara Thomas and plead for the return of the money. Swanny threw this man out of the house.

The suggestion was later made that Lee Kun got a raw deal, both before and after his trial, simply because he was not English. That racial prejudice might have been at work can be seen when looking at what befell Lee Kun's emissary after being physically mistreated by Clara Thomas latest boyfriend. After Swanny had thrown him into the street, the Chinese man blew a whistle to summon help from the police. They were on the scene promptly enough, but instead of investigating what was a clear case of assault, they arrested Lee Kun's friend and locked him in the cells for a few hours.

It is impossible to know what was going through Lee Kun's mind and the extent to which his subsequent actions were motivated by jealousy and how much of his anger was because he had been cheated out of his money. Whatever the reason, Lee Kun went round to see Clara Thomas for a final time on the afternoon of Saturday, 16 October 1915. Clara and Harriet Wheaton were sitting together in the front room, when there was a knock at the door. Swanny wasn't there and the two young women were alone in the house. Although she evidently had no wish to see him, Clara let him come in and her former boyfriend then asked if he might speak privately to her.

He took her by the arm and guided her into the backyard; out of earshot of Harriet Wheaton. Then there came the sound of a struggle, with scuffing of feet and faint cries. Harriet rushed out to see what was going on.

Lee Kun was stabbing Clara repeatedly with a large sheath knife. There was a lot of blood and, showing great bravery, Harriet snatched up a broom and tried to save her friend. The infuriated man then turned on her and she somehow managed to keep him at bay while screaming for help. Two passers-by came to her aid and succeeded in disarming Lee Kun, who was then arrested.

It was when he appeared at the Old Bailey before Mr Justice Darling that Lee Kun achieved immortality of a kind for advancing the most implausible defence ever heard at that court. His story was that he had left the house with Clara Thomas, only for her to produce unexpectedly a knife; with which she began to stab herself, with the obvious intention of committing suicide! Naturally, he did what any decent person would have done, which was to try and grab the weapon from her and protect her from herself. It was at this moment that Harriet Wheaton came on the scene and of course hopelessly misinterpreted what she saw. The whole thing was a terrible misunderstanding and Lee Kun was glad to have the opportunity now to set the record straight.

Readers may be taken aback to learn that the jury took less than half an hour to reject this ingenious explanation and that they had no hesitation in convicting the accused man of wilful murder. Although there can be little doubt that Lee Kun was indeed guilty of murder, it is also true that he seems to have got something of a raw deal from the British legal system. In the first place, his attempts to settle his dispute with Clara Thomas by appealing to the police were ignored. The police refused to become involved. The way that the case was reported in the press also suggests that race was introduced needlessly into considerations of the crime. It was the practice in those days to refer to murders by the geographical location: the Wimbledon Poisoning, the Hyde Park Murder and so on. In this case, the crime was defined by the ethnicity of the accused person. Newspaper headlines invariably referred to the 'Chinaman' or the 'Chinese murder case'.

It should perhaps be borne in mind that during the First World War foreigners of all types were viewed with suspicion by the British public as a whole. The Chinese were viewed as being especially cunning and prone to criminality, often having, into the bargain, an abnormal sexual desire for white girls. The first of Sax Rohmer's Fu Manchu books, *The Mystery of Fu Manchu*, had been published the year before the outbreak of war and the so-called 'Yellow Peril' was for many people an established fact. All of which meant that the jury at a trial of a Chinese man for the murder of a white girl was unlikely to be completely unbiased.

Despite the clear-cut and unequivocal evidence which had led to his conviction, Lee Kun's appeal in December looked as though it had an excellent chance of succeeding. His counsel, Tristram Beresford, pointed out that much of the proceedings during the trial at the Old Bailey were quite incomprehensible to the accused man. This was essentially a crime of passion and yet the impression given by the prosecution was that it was no more than a sordid squabble over money. The fact that the defendant sat impassively throughout the trial, his face seemingly expressionless, tended to reinforce the idea that this had been a cold blooded and heartless crime. The truth of the matter was that he had looked inscrutable purely and simply because he didn't understand for a lot of the time what was being said.

Another point that the barrister made was that it was at that time a legal requirement before sentence of death was passed for the judge to ask the accused person if he or she could give any reason why sentence should not be pronounced. Mr Justice Darling, knowing that Lee Kun's English was weak, had not troubled himself with this formality.

The judges dismissed the appeal, mainly on the grounds that all the evidence heard at the trial had already been translated into Chinese and that nothing had been said at the trial which had not already been discussed and translated during the committal proceedings at the magistrates' court.

John Ellis hanged Lee Kun on New year's Day 1916. The execution was notable for being the first carried out on a Saturday for over fifty years.

William Robinson: Condemned by a Letter to his Girlfriend

Hanged at Pentonville, 17 April 1917

Reading through the newspaper reports and transcripts of trials held a century ago, one often has the feeling that far more must have been going on in the case than we are now aware of. Take, for instance, the violence which flared abruptly outside the Sussex Stores public house in London's St Martin's Lane. Today, St Martin's Lane is in the heart of the West End theatre district, but in 1916, this part of St Martin's Lane around Seven Dials was a rough area to be drinking in.

Canadian soldier Alfred Williams was drinking with an attractive young woman called Margaret Harding. We have several witnesses to the events which took place in and outside the public house on the evening of 26 November 1916. which ended with the death of 35-year-old Alfred Williams. One of the men who gave evidence at the subsequent murder trial was Walter Henry Rhodes, who also happened to be drinking in the Sussex Stores that evening. Rhodes gave a statement to the police and then testified in court that he had seen the Canadian soldier drinking in the pub with a young woman. He saw another man hand the Canadian a roll of bank notes and shortly afterwards, Alfred Williams left the pub with Margaret Harding. Rhodes observed two men get up and follow the couple outside. Shortly afterwards, there was the sound of scuffling and breaking glass. Along with other patrons of the Sussex Stores, Rhodes hurried outside to see what was going on. The soldier he had seen leaving, was laying in the road, his head being cradled by the woman with whom he had left the pub. There was no sign of the two men who had left the pub after them.

Alfred Williams had been fatally wounded by a stab wound to his neck, right behind his ear. He died on the way to hospital. According to Margaret Harding, the men who had followed them after they had left, had simply walked up and begun a fight with the Canadian. One of them had drawn a knife and used that on the man with whom she had been drinking a few minutes earlier.

The police arrested two men for the murder of Alfred Williams. One was John Henry Gray and the other a former soldier by the name of William James Robinson, who had been invalided out of the army as a result of a wound which had left one of his legs four inches shorter than the other. Walter Rhodes and Maggie Harding both identified them as the men who had followed Williams from the pub. Both men were then charged with the murder of Alfred Williams.

The trial of William James Robinson and John Henry Gray began on 5 March 1917. The defence advanced by both the defendants was that this was a case of mistaken identity and they were neither of them in the vicinity of the Sussex Stores on that fateful November night. Walter Rhodes was emphatic though that these had been the two men he had seen leave the public house shortly after Margaret Harding and Alfred Williams. The pinning of the murder on Robinson was due to Margaret Harding's evidence; she alone being an eyewitness to the murder itself. At the end of the three-day trial, the jury decided that only one of the men should be convicted of murder and that the other was guilty of the lesser offence of manslaughter. William Robinson was accordingly sentenced to death, while John Gray was sent to prison for three years.

Because the convictions were based only upon the evidence of two eyewitnesses, both of whom had been drinking that night, it seemed possible that an appeal might be successful. There was no forensic evidence to link either of the men to the crime, no murder weapon had been recovered and, most important of all, neither of the convicted men had admitted any part in the killing of Alfred Williams. Both men appealed, but before that, shortly after he was lodged in the condemned cell at Pentonville prison, William Robinson wrote a letter to his girlfriend. It is worth quoting this at length, because seldom can any man in his position have made such a fatal error. He said:

> *Although I tell you now that I am guilty of the crime, I am quite satisfied with my sentence. I want to impress upon you and everybody else that it was not done for robbery but it was simply unfortunate. I took him for somebody else I had a row with on the previous day and I had no intention of killing him. I do not look for sympathy, for I do not deserve it.*

It was at that time the practice to copy all letters sent from prison and Robinson's communication to his girlfriend was no exception. It is no exaggeration to say that this letter probably hanged William Robinson.

The appeals of both William Robinson and John Gray were both held at the High Court on the same day, in the late March of 1917. Gray was exceedingly lucky, having his conviction quashed entirely and being set free on the spot. As Lord Reading said, when delivering his judgement:

*It is not necessary that a man, to be guilty of murder, should actually
have taken part in a physical act in connection with the crime. If he has
participated in the crime, that is to say, if he is a confederate, he is guilty,
although he has had no hand in striking the fatal blow. Equally, it must be
borne in mind that the mere fact of standing by when the act is committed is
not sufficient.*

Things were not to proceed to such a happy conclusion for William
Robinson.

Robinson's counsel was hamstrung by that damning letter, in which his
client actually admitted his guilt. Although William Robinson claimed that
he could not recall writing the letter and said that his mind had been in
turmoil when he first arrived in the condemned cell, he could not deny that
he had written and signed what was, in effect, a confession.

The barrister pleading Robinson's case tried an intriguing defence, which
was that in the first place his client thought that the man he had attacked had
been somebody else and that secondly, he had not meant to kill him. Neither
argument proved persuasive to the court, who rejected the appeal and sent
William Robinson back to the condemned cell. His execution was set for 17
April 1917.

On the afternoon of 16 April, John Ellis arrived at Pentonville prison. The
hangman knew that Robinson weighed 126 pounds and stood five feet and
three inches tall. He still needed to see the man for himself, so that he could
judge the strength of the neck muscles and adjust the drop he would be
given, if necessary. As he often did, Ellis disguised himself as a prison warder
so that he could observe the man he was due to execute without causing him
the distress of realising that he was being sized up by the hangman. The
Home Office table recommended a drop of just under eight feet for a man of
Robinson's weight, but John Ellis wanted to give him an extra four inches.
The doctor and under sheriff both refused to countenance this and in the
end, exactly eight feet was agreed upon.

The execution was scheduled for 9:00 am and a few minutes before this
time, the various officials were waiting outside the condemned cell. The
doctor entered first and asked if there was anything that Robinson wanted.
To his surprise, the man about to be hanged said that he wanted a smoke.
When the doctor reported this to the governor, the request was refused.

Ellis entered Robinson's cell as the hour of nine struck. The man he was to hang was sitting in an armchair and made no move to rise. Ellis grasped his left hand, whereupon Robinson at once stood up. Before his wrists were strapped behind his back, the condemned man shook hands with the two warders who had been watching over him in his cell, saying, 'Goodbye' to them. They wished him goodbye and Ellis fastened Robinson's hands behind his back. The little procession then moved towards the nearby cell containing the gallows. The man who was about to die walked firmly to the scaffold, although he limped badly, because one leg was so much shorter than the other. When he reached the trapdoor and saw the waiting noose, he stopped dead. John Ellis said, 'Come forward, please.'

Once he was standing on the trapdoors, Ellis pulled the white hood over the head of the man who was about to die. Just as he did so, Robinson looked him in the eyes and said in a firm voice, 'Goodbye.' As the rope was placed around his neck, Robinson spoke his final words, which were, 'God forgive me.' Everything now being ready, Ellis moved to the lever which operated the drop. He saw that Robinson was about to topple over, not because he was fainting, but purely and simply because one of his legs was so much shorter than the other. While he had been putting the rope around Robinson's neck, the hangman had been supporting the prisoner with his other hand, by gripping his arm. When this support had been removed, it was enough to cause the man to began leaning suddenly to one side. Deciding that the most human course of action would be to complete the execution as swiftly as possible, Ellis did not go back to Robinson and try to get him to stand up straight; he simply pulled the lever and sent the condemned man plummeting to his death. The post mortem found that William Robinson had died instantly from a broken neck.

Appendix I

The Executioners

Before the building of Britain's railway network in the nineteenth century, executioners were purely local, based primarily in one city or town. Once it became possible to travel across the country in a matter of hours, the need for so many different hangmen was obviated and one or two men could undertake to carry out executions in any city at a day or two's notice. The first such national executioner was William Calcraft, who hanged hundreds of men and women between 1829 and 1874. Although he lived in London, Calcraft would hang men as far afield as Dundee.

During the First World War, there were two executioners working in Britain: John Ellis (1874-1932) and Thomas Pierrepoint (1870-1954). Ellis was by far the most prolific hangman during this period, carrying out 32 executions to Pierrepoint's eight. Between 1907 and 1923, Ellis hanged a total of 203 people. Before that, he had assisted at the execution of a number of others.

Applying to become an executioner was done simply by writing to the Home Office and asking to be considered for the job, which Ellis did in 1901. He was accepted for training and in April of that year, he was invited to attend a course on hanging at London's Newgate prison. Following this, his name was added to the Home Office approved list of assistant executioners. His first appointment to assist at an execution was in December 1901, when he took part in a double hanging in Newcastle. As assistant executioner, Ellis' duties were limited to strapping the condemned person's ankles together, once on the trap, while the executioner himself placed the rope around the neck and pulled the lever which operated the trapdoors. For this, Ellis received £2.2s (£2.10p). This does not sound a great deal, but at a time that the average factory worker was earning only £1 a week, it provided a considerable boost to Ellis's income from his business as a barber. Later, when he was a chief executioner himself, he received £10 for each hanging, which was a very handsome sum at that time; equivalent to more than two months' wages for a labouring man. During the 16 years that he was a hangman, Ellis' earnings averaged out at £125 a year, which was a reasonable income in those days.

Although hanging hundreds of men posed no problem at all for John Ellis, it is thought that it was the experience of hanging two women which caused him to tender his resignation to the Home Office. The hanging of women in twentieth century Britain was very rare. Of the 147 women sentenced to death in this country from 1900 to 1964, when the death penalty was effectively abolished, all but 16 were reprieved.

Although Ellis had assisted at the execution of a woman in 1903, the first woman that he actually hanged was Edith Thompson, whom he executed on 9 January 1923. The whole process was extremely distressing, because the condemned woman had hysterics and then fainted. She was carried to the gallows and hanged without regaining consciousness. Worse still, the hanged woman haemorrhaged and there was a good deal of blood to deal with after the execution. It is known that Ellis was opposed on principle in any case to the execution of women and the episode upset him greatly. Nine months later, he travelled to Scotland to hang another woman: Susan Newell. She was the first woman to be executed in Glasgow for 70 years. A little over three months after the execution of Susan Newell, Ellis wrote to the Prison Commissioners, telling them that he was no longer prepared to carry out executions.

In the early hours of 25 August 1924, just eight months after retiring as chief executioner, John Ellis' wife was shocked to hear a shot. Hurrying downstairs, she discovered her husband sitting in a chair with a bullet wound to his jaw. He recovered from this injury and was subsequently charged with attempted suicide, which was at that time a criminal offence. When he appeared in court, John Ellis was given a conditional discharge.

For the next eight years or so, Ellis was prone to bouts of depression. Part of this was due to the fact that the Great Depression gripped the country and many men did not have money to spare for paying a barber to shave them or cut their hair. Business was poor. On the evening of Tuesday, 20 September 1932, the former hangman was sitting in the kitchen of his home, brooding and speaking to nobody. Without any warning, he jumped to his feet and snatched up an open razor laying on a shelf. He brandished this at his wife and daughter, shouting, 'I'll cut off your heads!' Understandably, they ran from the house. Ellis ran to the front door and cut his own throat, making two wide gashes across the carotid artery. He was dead before the police arrived.

It is ironic that a man who hanged so many men who used razors to commit murder and attempt suicide, should have used this same method to end his own life. There can be little doubt that his career as executioner, and in particular the hanging of two women in the same year, affected him badly and quite possibly led to his subsequent suicide.

The other official executioner during the First World War was Thomas Pierrepoint, uncle of Albert Pierrepoint, perhaps the most famous British hangman of them all. The Pierrepoints formed a dynasty, a little like the Sanson family of French executioners.

The first Pierrepoint to become an executioner was Henry Pierrepoint, who was trained in 1901, the same year as John Ellis. After assisting at a number of executions, Henry Pierrepoint carried out his first hanging in 1905. From the beginning, there was a good deal of ill-natured rivalry between Henry Pierrepoint and John Ellis. Henry's brother Thomas became a hangman a few years after his brother. In 1910, Henry Pierrepoint arrived at a prison drunk. Ellis was his assistant and Henry Pierrepoint ended up attacking him. This ended Pierrepoint's career as executioner and ensured that John Ellis and Thomas Pierrepoint were more or less enemies from then on, Thomas blaming Ellis for his brother being offered no more commissions for executions. When he heard that John Ellis had killed himself, his only remark was, 'He should have done it years ago!'

Although Ellis carried out the great majority of executions to take place in this country during the First World War, Thomas Pierrepoint lasted as a hangman for far longer than Ellis. He was carrying out executions from 1906 until 1946, hanging a total of 294 people; a record only exceeded by his nephew Albert.

The unknown members of First World War firing squads

A total of eleven men were executed by firing squad at the Tower of London between 1914 and 1916. We are never likely to know the names of any of the

77 men who carried out these executions; they having been drawn at random from various army units, mainly the 3rd Battalion on the Scots Guards. It was this regiment which was stationed at the Tower during the early years of the twentieth century.

The use of firing squads has its roots in various ancient practices which were designed to spread responsibility for the deaths of criminals throughout the entire community. The Biblical penalty of stoning to death is one such method of ensuring that no single person, such as an executioner, can be held to have killed a condemned man or woman. The Celts who lived in this country before the Roman invasions sometimes arranged for groups of archers to fire simultaneously at some victim and the martyr St Edmund died in this same way.

The first firing squads to operate in Britain, that is to say squads of soldiers armed with muskets who all fired at once at a man found guilty of some military offence, were seen during the English Civil War of 1642-51. A century later, this method of execution had become established as the accepted way of dealing with military crimes such as mutiny, cowardice and desertion. Questions were asked during the First World War as to why the Tower of London was thought to be the best and most appropriate place to conduct executions by firing squad. After all, there were a number of army barracks in the capital; why hold these grisly ceremonies in one the most famous tourist attractions? The answer is probably that there was a precedent for using the Tower for military executions and that the reason for the choice of this location lay in events which had taken place almost 200 years earlier, when three soldiers from a Scottish regiment were despatched in this way within the grounds of the Tower.

In 1743 there was widespread and growing unrest in Scotland, which was to culminate two years later in the 1745 rebellion led by Bonnie Prince Charlie. The Black Watch, a highland regiment, had been ordered to London so that they could be reviewed by King George II. Shortly before reaching the capital, a rumour began circulating, to the effect that they were to be sent to the West Indies and that bringing them south in this way was part of an English plot. The regiment mutinied and when they were eventually captured and disarmed, many were imprisoned in the Tower of London. Three ringleaders, two corporals and a private were court martialled and sentenced to death. Farquhar Shaw, Samuel Macpherson and Malcolm Macpherson were all shot by firing squad within the precincts of the Tower. These were to be the last executions in the Tower of London until Carl Lody's in 1914.

The procedure for an execution by firing squad had, by the outbreak of war in 1914, become standardised. A group of soldiers, typically eight, were chosen at random. Those choosing the men obviously made sure that those selected were reasonably proficient shots. Their rifles were loaded for them. Seven of the weapons had live rounds of ammunition in the chambers, while the eighth was loaded with a blank cartridge. This was, at least in theory, so that every member of the firing party could believe that perhaps he had fired the blank shot and consequently had no part in the execution. In reality, anybody who has ever fired a .303 rifle will know that the recoil is ferocious and quite different from the effect of firing a blank cartridge. All those who fired bullets at the prisoner would have been perfectly aware of their role; as would the one who discharged the blank.

Those about to be executed by shooting are almost invariably secured to some immovable object, to ensure that the target is kept still. This is as much in the condemned person's interests as anything else; clearly, a swift and painless death is desirable. This is only likely to be achieved with a stationery target. There are two basic methods of keeping the prisoner in place. On the one hand, he or she can be tied to a post. This can be an uncertain business, because the possibility exists that the condemned person will faint and hitting a moving target is far more tricky than firing at one which is immobile. For all the executions which took place at the Tower of London during the First World War, another procedure was adopted. The men were seated on ordinary wooden chairs, to which they were secured by leather straps. This meant that even if the man about to be shot fainted or was struggling, as happened in one or two cases, the chest would remain in the same position. This brings us to another interesting point.

The point of the body aimed at by British military firing squads has always been the chest. This seems so obvious as to hardly be worth stating and yet other countries have quite different views on the matter. When the Emperor Maximillian of Mexico was shot in 1867, for example, the firing squad aimed at his head, as was customary in that country during such executions. This will, under ideal conditions, kill just as effectively as shooting at the heart. There are two reasons why headshots of this kind were never favoured by the British army. The first is a practical point. The head is a smaller target than the trunk. Many soldiers called upon to kill a man in cold blood felt shaky and ill at ease. This inevitably affected their aim. There is all the difference in the world between shooting at an enemy in the heat of battle and putting a bullet through a man who is tied to a chair. The larger the target at which such a man is aiming, the less the chance of missing it entirely, if the aim should be a little disturbed. Then again, however securely a man may be fixed to a post or chair, his head may move from side to side or drop down unexpectedly, should he pass out through terror. The trunk of the body is easily fixed in one place, with less scope for mobility than the head.

The Executions

1914

11 August	Percy Clifford	Hanged	Lewes
4 November	Charles Frembd	Hanged	Chelmsford
5 November	Karl Lody	Shot	Tower of London
10 November	John Eayres	Hanged	Northhampton
10 November	Henry Quartley	Hanged	Shepton Mallet
12 November	Arnold Warren	Hanged	Leicester
23 December	George Anderson	Hanged	St Albans

1915

23 June	Carl Muller	Shot	Tower of London
15 July	Robert Rosenthal	Hanged	Wandsworth
30 July	Haike Janssen	Shot	Tower of London
30 July	Willem Roos	Shot	Tower of London
10 August	Walter Marriot	Hanged	Wakefield
11 August	Frank Steele	Hanged	Durham
13 August	George Smith	Hanged	Maidstone
17 August	George Marshall	Hanged	Wandsworth
10 September	Ernst Melin	Shot	Tower of London
17 September	Augusto Roggen	Shot	Tower of London
19 September	Fernando Buschman	Shot	Tower of London
26 October	George Breeckow	Shot	Tower of London
27 October	Irving Ries	Shot	Tower of London
16 November	William Reeve	Hanged	Bedford
1 December	Young Hill	Hanged	Liverpool
1 December	John Thornley	Hanged	Liverpool
2 December	Albert Meyer	Shot	Tower of London
22 December	Harry Thompson	Hanged	Wakefield
29 December	John McCartney	Hanged	Wakefield

1916

1 January	Lee Kun	Hanged	Pentonville
8 March	Frederick Holmes	Hanged	Manchester
29 March	Roger Haslem	Hanged	Manchester
11 April	Ludovico Zender	Shot	Tower of London
3 August	Roger Casement	Hanged	Pentonville
16 August	William Butler	Hanged	Birmingham
6 September	Daniel Sullivan	Hanged	Swansea
12 December	Frederick Brooks	Hanged	Exeter
19 December	James Hargreaves	Hanged	Manchester
20 December	Joseph Deans	Hanged	Durham

1917

21 March	Thomas Clinton	Hanged	Manchester
27 March	John Thompson	Hanged	Leeds
29 March	Leo O'Donnell	Hanged	Winchester
10 April	Alexander Bakerlis	Hanged	Cardiff
17 April	William Robinson	Hanged	Pentonville
18 April	Robert Gadsby	Hanged	Leeds
16 May	Thomas McGuiness	Hanged	Glasgow
16 August	William Hodgson	Hanged	Liverpool
18 December	William Cavanagh	Hanged	Newcastle
19 December	Thomas Cox	Hanged	Shrewsbury

1918

12 February	Arthur De Stamir	Hanged	Wandsworth
21 February	Joseph Jones	Hanged	Wandsworth
2 March	Louis Voisin	Hanged	Pentonville
5 March	Verney Asser	Hanged	Shepton Mallet
9 April	Louis Van Der Kerk-Hove	Hanged	Birmingham

Appendix III

The Mechanics of Hanging

O ne of things that readers might have noticed about the activities of hangman John Ellis, is that he seemed to be obsessed with the length of the drops which he gave condemned prisoners. At times he had disagreements with prison governors and doctors on this subject and was generally keen to give a longer drop than that recommended by the official Home Office guidance on the matter. To understand what was going on, it is necessary to examine the history of hanging in this country.

Of the two methods used in this country to inflict the death penalty during the First World War, one requires little explanation. A high velocity rifle bullet fired at short range into the human chest will cause appalling injury. The explosive decompression of the lungs, combined with the violent rupturing of the heart will bring about instantaneous death. A single bullet will wreak such havoc; the seven delivered simultaneously by a firing squad are most decidedly a case of overkill! In the case of hanging, things are a little more complicated.

The use of hanging as a means of execution became widespread in Britain during the Anglo-Saxon era, those centuries which followed the end of the Roman occupation and preceded the Norman Conquest in 1066. For a pre-industrial civilisation, the great advantage of hanging was that it needed little in the way of equipment other than a stout rope and a convenient tree. Later on, wooden frames were used for the purpose of hanging people; these became known as gallows.

For a thousand years or so, death from hanging was a painful and distressing business for the condemned man or woman. The victim choked to death agonisingly, with death taking anything up to half an hour to occur. This awful spectacle was thought to be salutary for the spectators; executions in this country being, until 1868, conducted in public. Not everybody subjected to this form of execution died of strangulation. Some fortunate souls had their necks broken, whether by accident or design, and so died almost at once. At Tyburn, for example, where hangings took place in London, the victims had ropes fixed around their necks while they were standing in a cart. When this was driven off, they were left hanging. Sometimes, the jerk of falling from the cart would be enough to fracture a person's neck and they would suffer a more merciful death than their fellows. It also happened from time to time that those about to be hanged contrived deliberately to die in this swifter way. When Guy Fawkes was being executed in 1606, he climbed the ladder and had the rope fixed round his throat. At this point, he summoned up all his strength and leaped into the air. The sudden jerk as the rope tightened, broke his neck and he died immediately.

In the early nineteenth century, a rudimentary mechanical gallows was developed, which dropped the condemned prisoner a short distance; typically a foot or two. Very rarely, this produced a quick death from a snapped neck, but the vast majority of victims still died from strangulation. In the early 1870s, a Lincolnshire cobbler called William Marwood had been giving a good deal of thought to technicalities of execution and devised what he thought would be a great improvement on the system then in use. Marwood believed that if a sufficiently long drop were to be given, perhaps between five and seven feet, then the neck would certainly be broken and the executed person killed instantly. On 31 March 1872, Marwood was allowed to carry out the execution of a man called Frank Horry. The hanging was a great success, in that Horry died at once, without any of the struggling which was a typical feature of hangings at that time. From then on, Marwood became the chief hangman in Britain and was evangelical in his advocacy of the so-called 'long drop'.

The authorities were very pleased with this new method of hanging, which made the whole process a lot neater and infinitely less upsetting for those whose duty compelled them to witness the hangings, which by this time took place only behind prison walls. What nobody other than the executioners themselves appeared to realise though was that this sort of hanging was an art, rather than a science. Autopsies showed that long drops of this kind caused death by fracturing the spinal cord, either between the second and third or fourth and fifth vertebrae; which may be seen in the X- ray photographs in Figure 7. To effect this neat and lethal injury, a striking force of a thousand foot-bounds must be delivered to the cervical vertebrae of the neck. Calculating the drop necessary to deliver this much force is a simple enough matter, but there is a little more to it than that. The condition of the neck muscles must also be taken into account, as must the age and sex; a muscular young man will need a greater drop than a middle aged woman, for instance. This meant that hangmen had to see their 'clients', in order to assess their physical condition and build. Ellis often went to great lengths to disguise himself when doing this, so as to spare the condemned man the a unnerving experience of being sized up by the hangman. He would frequently dress as a prison warder, so as to observe unobtrusively the men and women whom he was about to hang.

Getting the length of the drop precisely right is crucial if you wish to avoid two unfortunate extremes; both of which were fairly common in the early days of the 'long drop'. On the one hand you do not want to give your victim so short a fall that the neck is not broken; leaving the man or woman to choke slowly to death. On the other hand, and even more importantly, you do not wish to make the drop so long that the jerk actually separates the head from the body; thus decapitating the condemned person. This actually happened on a number of occasions in the late nineteenth century and led to the Home Office drawing up an official table of drops to be used for executions. Perhaps the worst case of this happening was the hanging which became known in the prison service as the 'Goodale Mess'.

James Berry, who inherited Marwood's role as chief hangman, was notoriously erratic with the drops which he gave. The result was that sometimes his victims were strangled and at other, even more horrific times, they were decapitated. About a quarter of the executions which Berry conducted were bungled in this way. The most gory incident took place during the execution of Robert Goodale in Norwich in November 1885. Goodale was a heavy man, he weighed over 15 stones, and was also very flabby, with weak muscles in his neck. James Berry always erred on the side of caution when it came to hanging people, preferring to give a longer drop than was strictly necessary, to avoid the chance of strangling somebody, instead of breaking their neck. At Norwich on 13 November that year, he was a little too generous with his drop. Whether it was because he didn't take fully into consideration the fact that Goodale had weak muscles in his neck or whether he had perhaps just miscalculated, the scene following the dropping of the man through the trapdoor was horrific in the extreme.

The horror began even before Goodale dropped through the trap with the rope around his neck. He refused to walk to the gallows and fought every inch of the way, screaming, fighting and struggling. Those present found it a relief when the prisoner's face was finally covered with a white hood, the noose adjusted and the lever pulled which would sent him hurtling to his death. The relief was short-lived however, because no sooner had Goodale disappeared through the trap, than the witnesses saw the rope flapping freely. It was at first thought that perhaps the noose had slipped over his head and that Goodale would have to be brought back up to the scaffold and hanged again. The truth was much worse. Robert Goodale's head had been pulled completely from his body and the decapitated corpse had spurted blood all over the whitewashed chamber beneath the scaffold. It was the worst mishap at an execution that anybody could remember.

Partly as a result of the 'Goodale Mess', a commission was set up under Lord Aberdare to look into the conduct of hangings and also the behaviour of the executioners themselves. There were stories of hangmen turning up at prisons drunk and others of the ropes used in the executions of notorious murderers being hawked around public houses and sold for so much an inch. The Aberdare Committee, whose official name was the Capital Sentences Committee, examined twenty-three executions and found that three had resulted in strangulation and two in decapitation; clearly an unsatisfactory situation. They accordingly drew up a table of drops which was adopted by the Home Office and was to be followed at all times by executioners in this country.

The problem with the table produced by the Aberdare Committee is that it took no account of the physical condition of the condemned prisoner and tried to impose a uniform length of drop based only upon the weight of the man or woman to be hanged. An experienced hangman was capable of using the table as the basis for his calculations and varying the length of the drop when necessary. It was this which caused John Ellis so many problems during the years of the First World War. Most governors did not wish to take any chances by authorising drops which differed in any way from those recommended in the Home Office table. Men like Ellis knew that when a man to be hanged was particularly muscular, young and active, then this would mean that the drop should be increased.

That John Ellis was right about the correct length of drops and the Home Office sometimes wrong, is shown by the fact that on several occasions when he was forced to stick rigidly to the Home Office figures, men were not given enough of a drop and died by strangulation, rather than having their necks broken. Sometimes Ellis was compelled to engage in a certain amount of cunning and subterfuge in order to give a longer drop when he felt it was called for.

Although there were one or two cases where, through adhering to the recommended drops too closely, men failed to have their necks cleanly broken, the converse never happened in any of the executions carried out by Ellis. Nobody ever had their head ripped off.

There was one further complication which from time to time occurred during executions by hanging and could result in the condemned person being strangled, rather than having his or her neck expeditiously snapped. The calculations about the length of drop given were very finely done; usually to within an inch or so. The drop given was predicated on the assumption that the prisoner would be standing upright, with the rope secured to the neck, and then plummet vertically through the trapdoors. If a drop of six feet was given, then it was vital that the body of the condemned person fell uninterrupted for the whole of that distance. Problems arose when the man or woman on the gallows fainted at the last moment. If somebody leaned to one side or began to collapse downwards, then the length of the drop could be reduced by as much as two or three feet. This meant in practice, that there was a chance that sufficient moment would not be built up and the neck would not break at the end of the fall.

In fact many people about to be hanged did indeed faint as they stood awaiting their deaths. So swift was the process of securing the noose, strapping the feet and pulling the lever to operate the trapdoors, that in the majority of cases, the worst that happened was that the person about to die leaned slightly to one side. This could result in injuries from the trapdoors, chiefly to the face. For instance, one of the first men to be executed during the First World War, Charles Frembd, fainted as the lever was pulled and as a consequence received a black eye as he struck the trapdoor when falling.

In the worst case of the kind to occur during the First World War, that of Arthur Stamrowsky, also known as de Stamir, in 1918, the faint caused the man to receive such a reduced drop that instead of his neck being broken, the condemned man choked to death.

Bibliography

Brandon, David and Brooke, Alan (2006): *London. The Executioner's City*, Stroud, Sutton Publishing

Browne, Gordon and Tullet Tom (1982): *Bernard Spilsbury: His Life and Cases*, London, HarperCollins

Clark, Richard (2009): *Capital Punishment in Britain*, Birmingham, Ian Allen

Duff, Charles (1928/2011): *A Handbook on Hanging*, Stroud, The History Press

Eddleston, John (2012): *British Executions – Volume 4, 1916–1920*, Bristol, Bibliophile Publishing

Ellis, John (1996): *Diary of a Hangman*, London, Forum Design

Evans, Stewart (2004): *Executioner. The Chronicles of a Victorian Hangman*, Stroud, Sutton Publishing

Fido, Martin and Skinner, Keith (1999): *The Official Encyclopaedia of Scotland Yard*, London, Virgin Books

Fielding, Steve (2008): *The Executioner's Bible*, London, John Blake Publishing

Fielding Steve (2008): *Hanged at Liverpool*, Stroud, The History Press

Fielding, Steve (2006): *Pierrepoint. A Family of Executioners*, London, John Blake Publishing

Honeycomb, Gordon (2014): *Dark Secrets of the Black Museum 1835–1985*, London, John Blake Publishing

Majoribanks, Edward (1989): *Famous Cases of Marshall-Hall*, London, Penguin Books

Melikan, R. A. (Editor) (2003): *The Trial in History: Domestic and International Trials, 1700-2000*, Manchester, Manchester University Press

Mitchell, Angus (2013): *Roger Casement*, Dublin, The O'Brien Press

Moore, William (1974): *The Thin Yellow Line*, London, Leo Cooper

Morton, James (2010): *Spies of the First World War*, London, The National Archives

Robins Jane (2011): *The Magnificent Spilsbury and the Case of the Brides in the Bath*, London, John Murray

Sellers, Leonard (2009): *Shot in the Tower*, Barnsley, Pen and Sword Books

Skinner, Keith (2006): *The Scotland Yard Files*, London, The National Archives

Thompson, Basil (1922): *Queer People*, London, Hodder and Stoughton

Tibballs, Geoff (2000): *Legal Blunders*, London, Constable and Robinson

Tullet, Tom (1979): *Strictly Murder. Famous Cases of Scotland Yard's Murder Squad*, London, Bodley Head

Webb, Simon (2012): *Execution. A History of Capital Punishment in Britain*, Stroud, The History Press

Index